TIM RICHARDSON

Futurescapes

DESIGNERS FOR TOMORROW'S OUTDOOR SPACES

With 472 illustrations

Thames & Hudson

Frontispiece: California Academy of Sciences,
San Francisco, by SWA Group.

First published in the United Kingdom in 2011 by
Thames & Hudson Ltd, 181A High Holborn, London WC1V 7QX

Copyright © 2011 Tim Richardson

Designed by Myfanwy Vernon-Hunt

British Library Cataloguing-in-Publication Data
A catalogue record for this book is available from
the British Library

ISBN 978-0-500-51577-8

Printed and bound in China by Toppan Leefung Printing Ltd

Contents

Introduction

This is a genuinely exciting period in landscape and garden design worldwide, with designers now possessed of a clear and urgent sense of purpose in the light of the global ecological situation, coupled with clients' new-found awareness of their ecological responsibilities. In the past decade, architects, too, have become far more open to the concept of working in tandem with landscape designers, while from a commercial point of view, corporate, civic and private clients are now more likely to include a landscape element as a significant part of the budget in new design projects. Within the landscape profession itself, a fruitful tension has arisen between those who now seek to include a clear ecological component in their methodology, and those who prefer to make reference to nature through their own mode of artistic expression.

Futurescapes consists of three main elements. At the heart of the book are the profiles – alphabetically arranged and including several hundred illustrated case studies – of fifty leading landscape companies from around the world. These range in size from large firms employing hundreds of staff to tiny companies with fewer than ten people, and in some cases just one individual. Every landscape company working in the world today has been assessed for inclusion, with the three watchwords being 'significant', 'distinctive' and 'innovative'. 'Potential' has also been taken into account. Company size or apparent commercial success have not been used as criteria. In addition, almost all of the work included has been completed within the last decade – most of it within the past few years – and there is no duplication between *Futurescapes* and its companion volume *Avant Gardeners* (Thames & Hudson, 2007), which also featured profiles of fifty landscape companies, focused in that case on the broad category of 'conceptualist' design.

Dispersed at intervals throughout the book are three essays on the topic of contemporary movements in outdoor-space design. These essays make special reference to the academic doctrine of 'landscape urbanism', now rebranded as 'ecological urbanism', and the popularity of landform as a design genre. In addition, *Futurescapes* features two 'forums', in which leading designers and critics have been invited to set out their personal visions of the challenges and opportunities now facing landscape designers.

The range of work on show in this book reflects the diversity of design in the contemporary landscape world; not everything will be to everyone's taste, but that is part of the point. What I hope sings out from these pages is a strong sense of the burgeoning creativity and individuality in landscape design in the first decade of the 21st century, a time that might be considered, given the environmental situation, landscape's 'moment'.

AGENCE TER

KARLSRUHE, GERMANY / PARIS, FRANCE

Innovative, interdisciplinary agency that sees no distinction
between landscape and urban planning.

Founded in 1986 by Henri Bava, Michel Hoessler and Olivier Philippe, Agence TER
now boasts a network of international outposts across Europe and the Middle East.
The stated aim of the firm is never to separate the discipline of landscape architecture
from urban planning. They work at the macro-scale – for example, with their projects
in northeast Paris, the renovation of Les Halles (also in Paris), and a new city in
Bahrain (with a population of more than 100,000) – but are also happy to undertake
smaller-scale commissions, even down to garden size. This unusual level of flexibility
emerges as the key to the company's identity, bound up with an approach to the work
that the partners describe as conceptual. 'The intrinsic qualities of the site and its possible uses,' they say, 'as well as the economic, social and political data relating to it, are
interpreted as part of a global concept, no matter what the scale of the job.' The designers state that there are three specific areas that recur in terms of importance and
emphasis in the projects they undertake: water, layers and horizons. The term 'layers'
here refers to Agence TER's predilection for cladding large areas of space with striking
or characterful materials to create a base from which to work, as well as, in a conceptual sense, to the layering of meaning.

    The Floorworks project (2005), a park around the offices of the Société Privée de
Gérance in Geneva, Switzerland, is emblematic of the 'layering' approach, in that a
single material, Corten steel, covers much of the surface of the 'park' space and is also
used to create a jagged jungle of tall metal spires and angular seats that erupts out of
the ground plane. This conceptual underpinning is a play on the term 'floorworks', in
that gardening is about 'working' the ground, or, in this case, 'floor', while both the

01

03

04

05

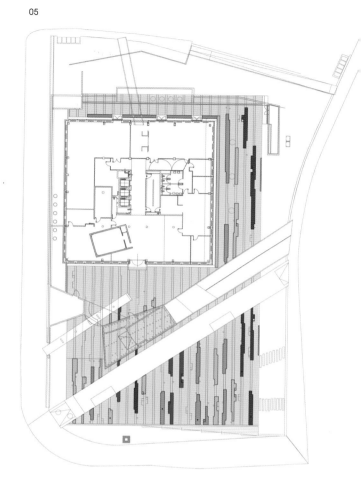

01 The co-mingling of naturalistic plantlife
and metallic forms works to good effect
at the Floorworks project in Geneva.
02 Grey slate pathways bisect the garden
and provide a contrast with the Corten
steel panels that cover most of the space.
Each of the metal spires is a unique shape.
03-05 Plantings of ornamental grasses disrupt
the linearity of the groundplan and create
variations in texture.

action and the result of the designers' efforts can also be called 'work'. The red-brown steel panels that constitute the 'floor' of the space are folded and distorted according to the topography and the structures they enclose. The edges of each panel have been cut and folded, creating 'figures' or spires, each one different in form but equal in height. These forms provide support for climbing plants, and can also act as seating. The living elements that animate the garden (the plants and running water) are found between the panels, where the folding and cutting process has left an uneven edge. The eastern and southern edges of the park are fringed with trees, while the forms themselves are planted with flowering perennial climbers, such as clematis, and with annuals that are renewed each year. Ramps of grey slate, crossing the garden or providing access to the offices, seem to float above the steel panels on the ground plane.

The Vache Noire project (2008) at Arcueil, near Paris, takes its unusual title from an area of the town that goes by this name, now undergoing significant commercial and residential development. Agence TER was commissioned to plan and landscape

06

06 At the Vache Noire development in Arcueil,
   giant glass and steel structures protrude
   from the landscape on the roof of a
   shopping centre.
07 The other-worldly landscape reflects the
   optimistic and innovative tone of this
   development.

various areas, including the 'rehabilitation of a roundabout' at Place de la Vache Noire.
Here, a stylized forest of mature Taxodium trees forms a kind of boundary around, or
a stage for, an area of artificial mist that creates a screen onto which a huge image of a
black cow is projected. Another intervention is a large park area, more than a hectare
(2.5 acres) in size, on the roof of a new shopping centre, which features a variety of
glass and steel structures with both practical uses (ventilation, air conditioning, and
so on) and a striking aesthetic quality. These structures feature panels of suspended
'vertical' planting and can be lit at night.

07

08-13 The Parc des Cormailles (2008) at Ivry-sur-Seine, also near Paris, is a new park constructed on ex-industrial land next to the railway lines. A huge mound of spoil was converted into a mound feature with a generally wilder feel than the rest of the park. The form and scale of the mound is echoed on the ground plane in the children's play area. The intention was to emphasize the general flatness of this part of the Seine valley, reconnecting the park with the town by means of the wide footpaths, while also creating a variety of different park and garden experiences.

11

12

13

BALMORI

NEW YORK, NEW YORK, USA

Award-winning landscape outfit that seeks to explore and expand
the boundaries between nature and structure.

Diana Balmori explores the potential links between the social function of public land-scape design, as inherited from the Modernist tradition, and the environmental and ecological imperative that has become urgently important in the 21st century. Balmori combines her design work with an academic career at Yale University, and is a senior fellow in garden and landscape studies at Dumbarton Oaks, Washington, DC. The firm's most important commission to date has been the masterplan for the waterfront development of the Abandoibarra district in Bilbao, Spain. The concept was to create a graceful, fluid aesthetic, weaving a landscape among the buildings of the industrial-ized city, thus linking the Old City with the new, developing centre.

Balmori has received a number of commissions in Bilbao. One of the most inter-esting has been The Garden That Climbs the Stairs (2009), on a site chosen by Balmori herself: a staircase between two towers designed by Arata Isozaki, leading to Santiago Calatrava's footbridge over the Nervión River. An amorphous planting bed appears to tumble down the steps, or gather itself at the foot of the stairs before creeping upwards. Balmori says of this piece: 'In one gesture, it narrates a story of landscape taking over and expanding over the public space and architecture, transforming the way that the stairs and the space is perceived and read by the user. It is a garden of contrasts: between native and exotic plants; the red flowers and the green grass; the green grass and the grey paving. In form, the garden engages the horizontal plaza with the rising vertical plane of the steps and the upright gesture of Eduardo Chillida's sculpture. Like the famous Spanish Steps in Rome, the garden is not only designed for visitors to ascend and descend, but for them to linger, and just be.'

01-03 The Garden That Climbs the Stairs in Bilbao is a strident landscape intervention in an area of the city noted for its signature architecture. Here, Balmori instigated a slightly subversive horticultural installation that smacks somewhat of 'guerilla gardening' – the spontaneous and often illegal gardening of public space in city centres that are otherwise devoid of greenery and signs of life.

01

02

03

07

04-06   The rooftop garden for 684 Broadway was
        conceived as a rich interpretation of living
        nature in one of the most densely urban
        environments conceivable. The complex
        series of levels and spaces that typifies
        such roofscapes is here used to create
        small, discrete parts of the garden, which
        are reserved for specific functions, such as
        showering, sunbathing, cooking and viewing
        the city.
07   The jaunty entrance plaza to Miami's
        Performing Arts Center is given a suitably
        glamorous treatment by Balmori, courtesy
        of dramatic lighting, geometric paving
        patterns and exotic planting.

At 684 Broadway (2007), a private residence in New York, Balmori created a large roof garden that integrates with an interior garden, lit by a 6m- (20 ft-) long skylight. A curtain of tall grasses encircles the rooftop living space, above which is suspended a bi-level ipe wood deck. On the lower level, a gravel path leads to a lookout pod with views over the Lower East Side, an outdoor shower and a more private enclave with jacuzzi and sunning deck, while on the upper level is an outdoor kitchen and lounging space. Birches punch through the deck, creating dappled afternoon shade. Quite different in tone is the glamorous entrance plaza to Miami's Performing Arts Center (2007), a space that links the opera house, symphony hall, theatre and Art Deco tower. Balmori clarified the spaces by introducing changing paving patterns. Rings of plants and fountain elements at the plaza's edge provide a transition between the street and buildings, which are elevated for flood protection. The palms and lighting help create a 'showtime' atmosphere, suitable to the purpose of the space. The dry 'fountain' sculpture, designed by Anna Murch, defines one end, drawing upon wave patterns to create a feature that lends animation to the design, even in the absence of water.

PATRICK BLANC

PARIS, FRANCE

Pioneer and leading exponent of the dramatic 'living-wall' concept.

With the creation of his first large-scale vertical garden in the courtyard of the Pershing Hall Hotel (2001), in Paris, the botanist Patrick Blanc established himself as the leading innovator and technical exponent of a highly irregular yet unfailingly striking branch of horticultural practice. Other high-profile gardens include those at the Musée du Quai Branly and the Fondation Cartier, also in Paris. Now these 'living walls' can be found all over the world, at museums, hotels, offices, residential developments, even an underground car park, with the designer juggling as many as six international projects at any one time. In the past decade or so, hundreds of vertical gardens have been constructed by other practitioners, inspired by Blanc's example, though in many cases the planting has failed because of inexperience or inadequate maintenance. Thus far, only Blanc appears to have mastered the technical issues; he has created patterned walls of burgeoning foliage that really do resemble gardens.

Blanc's argument is that plants do not need very much soil – or indeed, any soil – in order to grow well, provided they receive enough carbon dioxide, water, light and minerals. One of his 'secrets' is the discovery that these minerals can be absorbed via rainwater, which drips down through the plants on the upper levels and reaches those below. He came to this realization having observed how plants – including epiphytic plants, which grow above ground, attached to trees – survive and thrive in a rainforest environment. In order to avoid the damage to walls caused when plants grow directly out of the cracks and crevices of a building, Blanc devised his *mur végétal* methodology, comprising a system of fabricated pouches that are suspended on a strong framework. Because no soil is used, weight is kept to a minimum.

01

01–02 This project at Rue d'Alsace, in Paris (2008), was one of Blanc's largest to date. His plantings characteristically form great swathes of foliage in many shades of green.

03 The Caixa Forum (2007), in Madrid, is a city-centre set piece where artificial irrigation is a necessity due to the climate (the vertical wall is not the most 'eco-friendly' horticultural system). There are some 20,000 plants here, from about three hundred different species.

04 The arched entrances to the tunnel beneath the Pont Max Juvenal (2008) in Aix-en-Provence, in southern France, were decorated by Blanc in dramatically linear fashion.

04

The pockets are made of a kind of felt material (a surface suitable for the plants' root systems), up to about thirty plants per square metre (or 11 sq ft), allowing for dense plantings equivalent to those found at ground level. Another crucial element is the fact that the structural frame is kept 1m (3 ft) away from the existing building wall, thus allowing air to circulate. An automated system provides water and nutrients that are distributed from the top level, and then drip down through the entire structure. The system can be realized on any scale, both indoors and out. Technical issues aside, Blanc is adept at creating swirling abstract patterns of plant material across the façades of buildings, in single, rectangular blocks that appear as painted canvases of living pigments, in a surprising range of colours, or on façades with fenestration, where the living plantings create a strong sense of individuality in an urban context.

CHRISTOPHER BRADLEY-HOLE

LONDON, ENGLAND

Modernist garden designer who combines elegant architecture
with naturalistic plantsmanship.

Having made his name in the 1990s creating sleek, minimalist spaces, Christopher
Bradley-Hole has recently turned to the possibilities of naturalistic planting and how
it might intersect with the Modernist aesthetic. He has been highly influenced by the
New Perennials school of planting (see Piet Oudolf; p. 206), favouring the repetition
of grasses and sculptural perennials across large areas of planting. His style is a sophisticated development of the early realization experienced by Modernist designers
(including Christopher Tunnard and Le Corbusier) that a naturalistic planting style
suits modern architecture, partly because of the simple contrast between smooth and
'shaggy', and partly because it expresses something of the idealization of form evinced
in buildings of this genre. A typical garden design unites formalist rigour with exuberant yet carefully planned drift plantings of grasses and perennials, such as rudbeckias
and echinaceas. At several gardens, Bradley-Hole has taken this methodology to its
logical conclusion in formalist terms by creating a simple grid of planting squares,
designing each individually, yet allowing for rhythms and echoes to develop between
them. The result is a burnished, moving ocean of plants, awash with colour. Bradley-
Hole's style is also wedded to the clients' needs: whether or not they have children; if
they are keen horticulturists; what times of day they like to use the garden. It is his
attention to detail, both in planting and in hard materials, which has become his
trademark, a characteristic that he ascribes to his Modernist background.

At Crockmore House (2002), in Oxfordshire, Bradley-Hole utilized the grid-bed
system that has become something of a signature for him. From above, the gridded
pattern appears blurred into indistinctness. This is especially true in summer and

01 The gridded garden space at Crockmore House, in Oxfordshire, where Bradley-Hole created an impression of seamless transition as the planting schemes 'jump' across the dividing paths.

02   03

autumn, when the plants have grown up (notably the miscanthus and stipa grasses that form the planting structure), but it is a rigorous underlying aesthetic, with each bed exactly 2m² (22 sq ft). In this case, the grid is laid out next to an old orchard, where the contents of each square bed seem to echo or pre-empt the next in a sea of plants that is ablaze with golds, blues, purples and reds. The rich ornamental planting utilizes a palette of species that includes eupatorium, *Agastache foeniculum*, pink *Dianthus carthusianorum*, purple *Aster x frikartii* 'Monch', *Lysimachia ephemerum*, *Digitalis ferruginea* and the stately spires of *Veronicastrum virginicum* 'Album'. Beyond the eighteen beds of perennials are two rows of fruit trees, set in a formalized wild-flower meadow, and then a series of raised beds for vegetables, screened off by a beech hedge. The stylish treatment of the deck next to the house is glamorous as well as practical, with the smooth timbers offset by encroaching foliage, and a planted bank descending to the garden proper. The ensemble is modern without being reduced to the clichés of retro-Modernism.

04

05

02-05 For the Old Rectory in East Sussex,
the planting plan was simpler and more
repetitive. Bradley-Hole is a designer
who instinctively responds to the house's
architecture when planning gardens,
forging a creative relationship between
the two entities.

At a walled garden for a rectory (2007) in East Sussex, Bradley-Hole again used the grid structure as the basis for his design. Here, the planting was kept to a minimum, with a pared-down palette of plants that have been simply repeated from bed to bed, in more or less the same position. Among the key plants were calamagrostis grasses, *Stipa gigantea*, and two species of miscanthus, sinensis and gracillimus. The Manor House (2007), in Oxfordshire, saw Bradley-Hole working in minimalist mode; he says his key influence with this project was the Mies van der Rohe-designed Barcelona Pavilion, which featured a series of walls that never meet, so that exterior spaces were implied. He also wanted to create an impression of space on a small plot by devising simple, clean spaces, divided by hedges. And at a large walled garden (1999) at Bighton, in Hampshire, Bradley-Hole envisaged a series of 'contemporary parterres', made up of a grid of fifty-eight separate planting beds. Next to the house, he used the grid in a different way, planting squares of yew on one side and box on the other, as a direct response to the geometric fenestration of the Georgian building.

06–08 The Manor House in Oxfordshire was conceived in minimalist spirit, making the most of the space available by means of a simple, pared-down treatment.

09–10 At Bighton, in Hampshire, Bradley-Hole responded to the neoclassical architecture by adding a pair of hedged 'parterres', which echo the house's fenestration. Meanwhile, in the large walled garden, the designer produced his signature style of gridded beds planted exuberantly with grasses and perennials.

09

10

BRUTO

LJUBLJANA, SLOVENIA

Exciting young company with an exuberant
and unpredictable signature style.

Matej Kučina is principal landscape architect at Bruto, a company he founded in 2004, having previously worked with Peter Walker in California and as a partner at Scapelab, another Slovenian landscape office. Working with just two other landscape architects, Kučina has realized an impressive range of work in a short time, from residential garden projects to public parks and waterfronts. 'We don't differentiate between our tasks,' he says. 'It is important that the task is clearly defined and logical, whether it is a garden or a multi-functional urban space.' He envisages landscape design that is 'complex, colourful, useful and alive', saying that 'it is more important how it works than how it looks'. The work is characterized by the great sense of clarity, and the bold use of formal outlines to define spaces and delineate function.

At the General Maister Memorial Park (2007), in Ljubno ob Savinji, Kučina formulated his groundplan as an abstract representation of the topography of the northern border of present-day Slovenia, where Rudolf Maister and his soldiers fought against the Austrian army in 1918–19 (the park is dedicated to the general and his men). It was planned as an abstract three-dimensional space, where paths lead around geometrically cut grass crests, next to the river. The crest adjacent to the road is truncated and terminates in a supporting wall, which serves as a part of the memorial; on it is a line of bronze sticks, bearing the names of Maister's soldiers. The symbolic composition concludes with a life-sized equestrian statue in bronze.

Cufar Square (2003) in Jesenice, also in Slovenia, is the most important public space in the town, surrounded as it is by key buildings that include a school, a cinema, a theatre and a library. The goal of the design was to create a multi-functional space

01

01 At the General Maister Memorial Park, Bruto created an artificial topography using geometric grass mounds that echo the shape of the mountains of the northern frontier of Slovenia, where the general and his men fought in 1918–19.

02–04 The bold ground patterning at Cufar Square is what marks the project out in terms of confidence and panache from much other contemporary urban design.

that could serve as a city square, and also as a concert and public area. The central part of the square is dominated by a computer-controlled fountain of vertical jets, which create a variety of patterns. While this is now something of a cliché of public-space design, the originality of the project lies in the bold, black-and-white groundplan, which extends across the whole square. An adjacent terrace can be used as a performance area, while the square itself becomes an auditorium.

The new Wellness Orhidelia (2009), at Podčetrtek, typifies the imaginative exuberance of Bruto's work. The centre is situated in the densely built-up area of the Olimia health resort and hotel complex. This colossal facility is entirely built below ground, so the whole of the ground-level area is arranged as an urban park. Slopes, stairs and terraces are linked to the various subterranean hotels and baths of the complex. The main elements of Bruto's landscape design are a series of paved entrance squares, a lush pathway that leads across the roof of the underground building, wooden terraces that sweep gently down to the open-air pools, and the green areas of the roof. Bruto describes the result as 'simple and functional'. It is also excitingly geometric and materially inventive throughout.

03

04

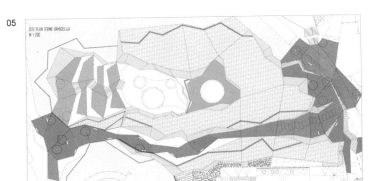

05 SITE PLAN TERME ORHIDELIJA
M 1:200

05-10 The new wellness centre at Podčetrtek incorporates subterranean hotels and baths, allowing Bruto to create a connecting design of striking linearity at ground level. One startling intervention is the wooden terrace that leads down to the grey and pink outdoor baths.

06

07

08

09

FERNANDO CARUNCHO

MADRID, SPAIN

Philosophically inspired designer of elegant and highly
original spaces on all scales.

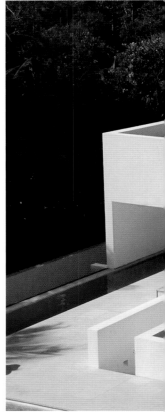

01

One of the most respected landscape designers working today, Fernando Caruncho specializes in large-scale formal designs in both the public and private spheres – mainly in his native Spain, but also increasingly farther afield. His earlier work was predicated on the idea of the grid form, a strongly geometric basis that allowed him to extrapolate into the natural world through the use of a limited palette of trees and, in several earlier projects (including the celebrated Mas de les Voltes), agricultural elements such as wheat fields. 'Geometry is man's first language,' Caruncho says. 'The oldest piece of signing in history is a deer bone engraved with straight lines.' He points out that people have always ordered and engaged with the landscape through geometry, notably in the Spanish gardens of Granada and Córdoba, where decorative patios are quartered by water rills, and in the Japanese garden-design tradition.

01-03 The Boca Raton garden in Florida was where Caruncho first departed from his habitual use of the grid form as a basis for design. The motif of interlocked circles arose spontaneously on the drawing board, and decisively altered the designer's entire output from that point on.

In recent years, Caruncho has relinquished the grid form as the basis for his work, and has become interested instead in the circle as an underlying form. Generally this is expressed in one simple, bold stroke, not dissimilar to the spiral that can be found in representations of the Golden Section, from Vitruvius onwards. Indeed, it is the classical world that emerges as the wellspring of Caruncho's design work, first discovered when studying philosophy at Madrid University. Of this process, Caruncho states: 'Returning to my studies of the first philosophers, the Pre-Socratics, I understood that today, more than ever, we need to study the essential elements of the universe. This is not so much the physical–chemical composition, more the mythical–spiritual relationship of man and the universe, and the potential for transforming man's spirit. From this moment, "transformation" became a key word for me, which I kept on the shelves of my heart with great devotion and respect: transformation,

04

transmutation, metamorphosis. Through this concept, I could see how the different and contrasting trends of rational and mythical thinking, from our Greek childhood, would flow through the "rosy-fingered dawn" and "wine-dark sea". It was this discovery, and this evidence, and this way of being and feeling, that made me decide to transform, transmute and undergo the metamorphosis from young philosopher to ancient gardener. I say "gardener" because this mythical word belongs to mankind and contains memories of our purest origins, so full of resonance and touching aspects both elemental and fragile. Not for nothing was a garden the first domain that the gods gave us, and in it we keep the memories and sacred images that will always take us back to this beginning.'

The Boca Raton project (1999), 15km (9 miles) north of Miami, Florida, represents a watershed moment in Caruncho's output, where a traditional Modernist 'white-cube' house by Ricardo Legoretta is complemented by a garden planned as interlocking circles: a circular pool with a shallow amphitheatre; grey pebbles laid around the pool; bougainvillea for colour; and three carefully chosen sculptures from the clients' collection. 'Previously you saw the grid form all the time in my work,' Caruncho explains, 'but at this time I began to see the space in terms of circles. It transformed my vision. It was a new geometry: I discovered the circle in the middle of

04-05 On a smaller scale, the Palatchi garden was conceived as one simple move: a long, powerful curve of path and hedge, encircling a central grove of jacaranda trees on the lawn and culminating in the swimming pool below.

the grid. My vocabulary and grammar developed, and I felt I began to understand more. I discovered, when I was first working on this project, that my hand made two circles on the paper, and I said to myself, "This is not possible." I was afraid. Twenty minutes later I understood that it was not banal. My hand understood more than my brain.' Caruncho says his own team was initially unsure about this transition from a square to a circle, but it now dominates his own thinking. The design for the Palatchi garden (2004), in Barcelona, is, like the Boca Raton garden, also based on a simple, swirling form: a ramp accompanied by a substantial hedge that sweeps down towards a pool, which is a continuation of these forms. A grove of jacaranda trees in the middle of the garden creates form, colour and a sense of purpose for the small-scale space.

Caruncho describes the Silva garden (1997) in Madrid as 'my last garden before the circle – it was the most strictly gridded garden of all, and it formed a link with what came next'. This garden of low ramps, sheerly clipped hedges and pools is predicated in the idea of a carpet, in the classical parterre tradition. The impact and presence of the sky is extremely important here, as it is in many of Caruncho's designs. 'For me, this relationship between the sky and the land is most important,' he says. 'In the equation of landscape, I tend to lose more garden and allow more sky.' An old evergreen oak was retained at the centre of the space, and Caruncho describes the

06-08 'A magic carpet' is how Caruncho describes the Silva garden in Madrid, in that it is conceived as transcendent space because of (rather than despite) its severe geometry. The design is focused around an old evergreen oak, while maples light up the space in autumn.

09 The Cotoner garden in Majorca utilizes a simple palette of plants: alternating olive and cypress trees, backed by hedges of *Pistacia lentiscus*, around a central pool.

whole design as a dialogue with this characterful tree. It is also a magical place of escapism, in that a magic carpet can transport one away from reality. Acers at the edge of the garden help light up the space in spring, summer and, of course, autumn.

The Cotoner garden (1994) in Majorca also dates from Caruncho's 'grid' days: a garden clearly in thrall to the classical (that is, 17th-century Baroque) traditions of Spanish architecture and garden design, specifically in this case the gardens of the Royal Alcázar palace in Seville, which also features a pavilion that 'floats' in a large lake. Surrounded by fields of wheat, lemons and pomegranates, Caruncho calls this a 'farm garden'. The main design idea is extremely simple: the alternation of olive trees and cypress trees around the central pool, backed by multiple hedges of *Pistacia lentiscus*. The contrast of form and colour, in the context of the wider landscape, proves to be all that is necessary to make a dignified and appropriate design here.

Caruncho is currently working in New Zealand, and is also undertaking his first commission in Britain – a minimalist design around an old stone house in the Cotswolds, with the remains of a terraced garden.

09

10 At the Madrid Botanic Garden (2005), Caruncho was tasked with redesigning a forgotten and unused corner of the garden, where it meets the Retiro Park on a steep slope. The space was reconceived as an area for the display of bonsai specimens of native trees, the collection of ex-president Felipe González. Caruncho introduced the elegant limestone steps and the 'green walls' of myrtle and laurel.

11 The long ramp or 'tongue' of a cobbled walkway leads down one level towards the entrance to the glasshouse.

12 An elliptical pool provides a focal point, where visitors can sit among the bonsai. Caruncho's plan is to introduce niches that are decorated in gold leaf, better to show off the bonsai specimens.

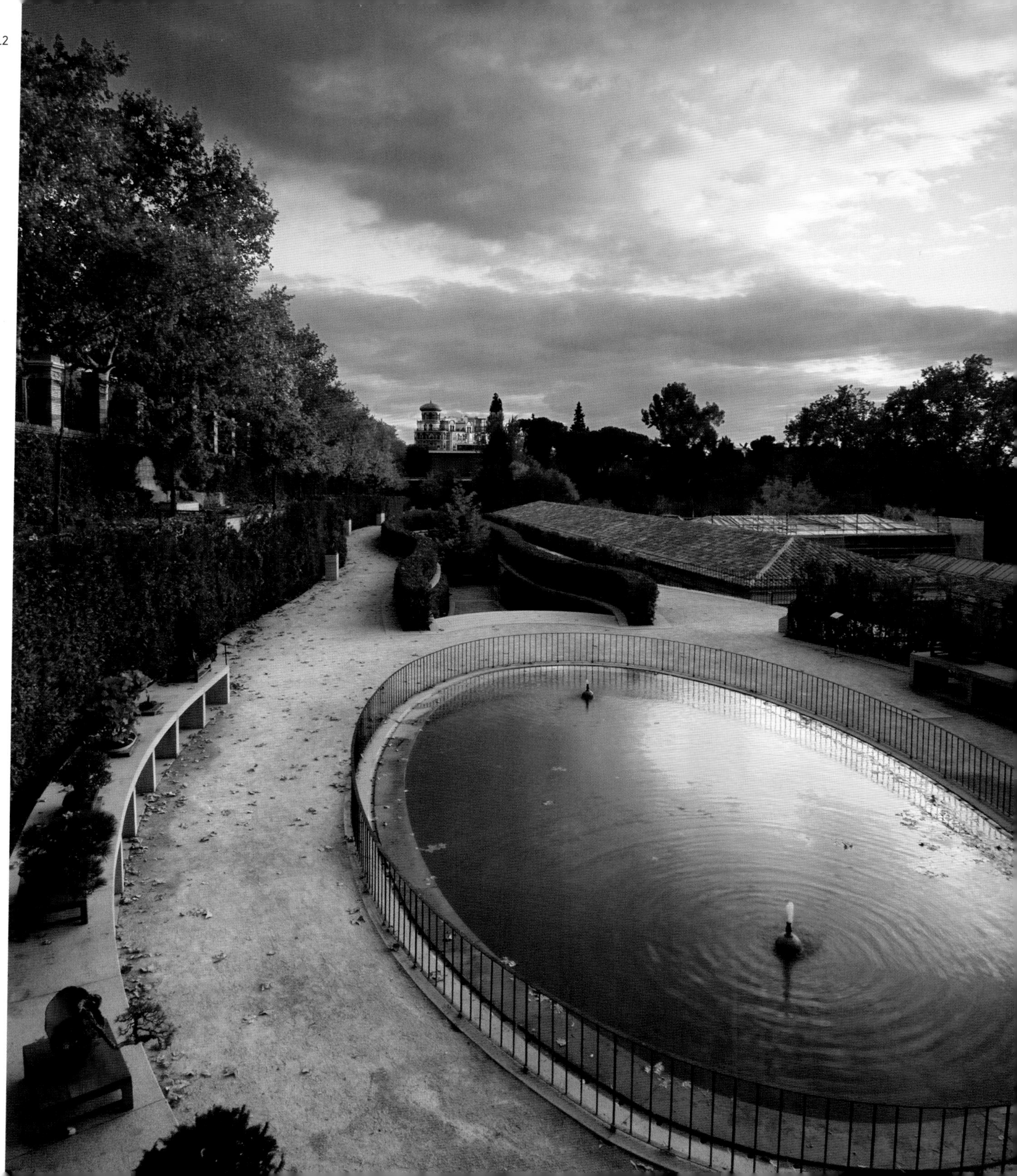

ANDREA COCHRAN

SAN FRANCISCO, CALIFORNIA, USA

A designer working within the traditions of Californian Modernism, with the addition of bold, painterly plantings and strident sculptural interventions.

Initially apprenticed to the Modernist architect Josep Lluís Sert on the East Coast, Andrea Cochran's style developed in the minimalist warp and weft of the landscape-architecture culture of California. Her work superficially resembles that of Dan Kiley and, to a lesser extent, Thomas Church, though its sculptural quality is somewhat bolder, especially when realized on a larger scale. It is a broadly minimalist approach, with conceptualist flourishes. Other key influences have been the work of Luis Barragán, in terms of the progression of spaces through a landscape and in the internal clarity of individual episodes, and of André Le Nôtre. It is perhaps better to understand this last influence less in terms of design specifics and more as a realization among young designers travelling in Europe for the first time that 'empty' space is a tactile and malleable element, which can and must be worked with on every scale. It appears the example of Le Nôtre gave those working in the Modernist tradition in the second half of the 20th century a kind of 'permission' to work in a minimalist way (though Le Nôtre's work in its original form was in no sense minimalist).

A typical Cochran design will utilize space in an extremely active way, with a strong sense of rhythm within and between the spaces. The groundplan usually appears as severely linear, but the red-brown of Corten steel (a favourite material) and the various hues of stone are warming, while the planting style is often verdant and exuberant, if spare in terms of plant selection. Panels of green lawn give on to grids of trees (often European olives or maples) and reflective pools, while expanses of 'neutral' grey gravel constitute the ground plane, often juxtaposed with larger aggregates, boulders, or smooth-textured, low walls made of lighter-coloured stone.

01

01 The 30.5m- (100 ft-) long pyramid at Stone
   Edge Vineyard in California has no function
   other than as a screen, a meditative focus
   and balance to the two buildings created
   on site.
02 The observatory and library is surrounded
   by a 30cm- (12 in-) deep reflecting pool,
   overhung by the striking large cape rush,
   Chondropetalum elephantinum.
03 The meadow provides a coherent context
   for the 'trilogy' of structures, while also
   acting as an environmental means of coping
   with flooding.

At Stone Edge Vineyard (2007), in Sonoma, California, Cochran was asked to create a spa environment with a landscape garden on a 1.2-hectare (3.5-acre) site, an extension to a commercial vineyard that is also a private home. The ambitious specification included the spa building itself, as well as a lap pool and an observatory (the client is an astronomy enthusiast). The three main architectural features – spa, observatory and pyramid sculpture – were conceived by Cochran as a 'trilogy' to be connected and mediated by the water elements: the lap pool and the reflecting pool in which the observatory sits. The tone for the space is set less by the buildings than by the allées of mature olive trees and the adjoining drought-tolerant meadow. Designed as a monolithic mass, the meadow is made of four layered grasses – pink muhly, *Atlas fescue*, slender veldt and little bluestem – whose narrow leaves emphasize a graceful verticality. The plants were selected for their low water-use, while varied times of seed production highlight subtle seasonal changes throughout the year. Existing trees, such as old California bays, were retained and help create an atmosphere of permanence and solidity. Due to the proximity of the site to a nearby creek, careful consideration

03

04

was given to the development of a grading plan that would absorb potential flooding. A flood occurred during the project's construction, devastating the estate, and ultimately reinforced the design identity of the meadow as a wash to absorb flooding from the creek. It was also intended to heal and breathe new life into land damaged by the construction process. The most striking feature in the design is a low, asymmetrical, pyramid-shaped stone sculpture, 30.5m (100 ft) in length, which concludes the view in one direction down the lap pool. It is a looming yet benign feature, whose presence inspires meditation. Built from the native alluvial stones that were unearthed during construction, the sculpture arose out of a desire to reclaim local materials in an innovative way. It also acts as a visual screen, engendering a sequestered sense of privacy. Overall, there is a ritualistic atmosphere to this space that is not inappropriate in the context of spa activities and astronomical investigations.

04 The lap pool is focused on the pyramid, while flanking it is the observatory, with external staircase, and an ancient Californian bay tree.
05 Allées of gnarled old olive trees lend great character to a new landscape.
06 The buildings have a low-key presence, in balance with the trees, meadow and water.

05

06

VLADIMIR DJUROVIC

BROUMANA, LEBANON

Luxurious, clean-lined garden spaces and pools for an
uncompromising but beautiful climate and environment.

The work of Vladimir Djurovic's practice, founded in 1995, is sleek and modernistic, with a feeling of glamorous privacy. Most of the firm's commissions have been in Lebanon, Saudi Arabia and the United Arab Emirates, though Djurovic now also works extensively in Europe and North America. The work is unashamedly luxurious, with a private-client base composed almost entirely of the wealthy élite. The firm's signature is the use of elemental materials such as water – always as smooth sheets – and fire. As Djurovic says: 'Our work always modulates to capture and complement the spirit of the environment, but never deviates from being simple and reduced to its essence.'

In projects such as the residence of renowned fashion designer Elie Saab (2001), in Faqra, Lebanon, the design is formulated as an escape from the hectic lifestyle of the fashion world and as a venue for hosting parties. Withstanding severe climatic conditions at an altitude of 2,000m (6,561 ft), the landscape programme comprises a sequence of four spaces. The entrance approach consists of a main door, preceded by a 6m- (20 ft-) high wooden enclosure, which is raised to cope with the winter snowfall and to compensate for the limited planting depth. Large oak trees were used to frame the house and provide privacy from the street, while stone steps with recessed lighting connect the levels. The design of the upper terrace was intended to imply continuity from interior to exterior by means of a subtle paving pattern that is used throughout, though 'grooves' of grass are interpolated in the areas that are farthest from the house, and therefore closer to nature. The balustrades have been lowered and transformed into wide planters to provide an uninterrupted view of the mountains, and provide

01

02

for overflow seating during major events. The side garden, a simple maple forest, offers a sense of calm and privacy, acting as a solid screen between the house and main road, and allows for overspill from events on the upper terrace. The lower terrace is the heart of the garden: two simple rectangles, one a raised mirror of water (a swimming pool), the other a flat terrace with two recessed sitting areas with fireplaces. Panoramic views can be enjoyed across this plane of water by those seated within.

For a private client in Jiye (2006), also in Lebanon, Djurovic was initially asked to create a private spa area with indoor pool, plus an outdoor pool and entertainment area. Early on in the project, the client decided to change the brief so that the spa complex and entertainment area became a substantial residence with two separate wings. Djurovic's initial plan was to contrast the smooth-cut Travertine stone used for the floors and walls of the building with areas of rough-cut stone and boulders. Giant rocks excavated from the site were used for cladding the exterior walls of the spa, and

01 On the lower terrace at the Elie Saab residence in Faqra, a pair of sunken 'rooms' with central fireplaces provide space to enjoy the sunsets, while contemplating the simple rectangle of water that is the pool.

03

were then wrapped into the indoor spaces to provide a sense of continuous flow between interior and exterior. 'The sheer size of the rocks', says Djurovic, 'creates a primitive, cave-like experience for users,' who become pampered troglodytes in this other-worldly environment. The 'cave-like' spa is replete with meditation areas, massage rooms, a wet zone, a gymnasium and an indoor pool that seems to hover between indoor and outdoor space. Adjacent to the indoor spa pool is a 60m- (197 ft-) long outdoor swimming pool with an entirely different character: bright, blue and open.

ESTUDIOOCA

OFFICES WORLDWIDE

A truly international company, specializing in urban design and transportation, and not afraid of big gestures.

Branding itself as a specialist in 'urbanism and landscape' (in that order), estudioOCA has offices in Los Angeles, Barcelona, São Paulo, Marseille and Marrakech, with plans to open another location in Bangkok. Senior partners Ignacio Ortínez and Bryan Cantwell head up the branches in Barcelona and Los Angeles. In common with other firms that describe themselves as urban designers, or urbanists, estudioOCA markets itself partly on an ability and desire to work on many different scales: 'We work with a team of collaborators from various disciplines such as architects, engineers, landscape architects and environmentalists to provide solutions to the most complex landscapes. This formation allows the studio to work at all scales, from small-scale urban landscape interventions to large-scale redevelopment and masterplanning.'

Transportation is a particular specialism of the company, specifically what they describe as 'the intersection of transportation and public landscapes'. Modes of transport have emerged as a particularly important aspect of the work of many landscape designers in the past decade, partly as a result of the ecological imperatives that have affected local governments and city authorities. An important aspect of estudioOCA's work is the design of complete streets through the development of detailed streetscape designs and masterplans. These include bicycle lanes and facilities, together with what the firm describes as 'enhanced pedestrian experiences'. In Madrid, for example, the studio posited a project entitled Three Urban Itineraries – landscaped walking routes through interesting sections of the city. Urban designers today frequently find themselves kicking against the legacy of the 20th-century regime of the automobile.

01

01 The proposed design for a park in Madrid's
Parque de Valdebebas development includes
various stylized evocations of the natural
environment of this part of Spain, including
areas of indigenous trees and 'canyons' that
double up as places for seating.

02 The proposed Wetland Plaza, which evokes and honours the natural environment of the park.
03 The 'amphitheatre', formed by the largest of the park's three canyons, will offer locals a striking taste of nature amid a shiny, new residential and commercial development, whose form is essentially grid-like.
04 The natural topography of the site will be manipulated and exaggerated to create a memorable aesthetic experience, as well as a sense of release into nature, as here with the Mirador del Paseo.

04

03

EstudioOCA's proposal for an 80-hectare (198-acre) park in Parque de Valdebebas (ongoing), a vast commercial and residential development in northeast Madrid, provides a direct link to the existing park through a wide urban promenade, lined with an allée of native trees, and consisting of a café, abundant seating, petanca courts and bicycle-rental stations. The promenade slices through the topography at the western end, with the void creating a large overlook at the highest point of the site. The motto chosen for the competition, 'Regenerative Landscape', defined the concept. Through the manipulation of the existing topography and natural drainage systems, a series of three canyons were created, providing attractive space and creating wildlife corridors, which could develop and expand through the creation of micro-habitats.

North of the promenade is a large amphitheatre set on the edge of the canyon, nestled in native woodlands. Combining nature with engineering, through more natural bio-engineering techniques, a drainage system at the bottom of the canyon collects storm-water run-off from the northern half of the site, filtering the water as it flows towards the Wetland Plaza at the northeast corner of the site. South of the promenade are two smaller canyons, both based on the original drainage patterns of the landscape and ending at the Wetland Plaza. The plan is for the open areas to be restored with natural woodlands, modelled on those found in this part of central Spain. The perimeter area is a transition zone between the urban and the natural, containing plazas, cafés, playgrounds and sports facilities, all set within a grove of trees. At the south perimeter is a large transit zone that provides access to public transportation, along with a car park in an orchard setting.

THE CHALLENGE OF
LANDSCAPE URBANISM

In an era of competing ideologies, what is the future for landscape design? First, it is clear that the perceived global ecological crisis – enthusiastically marketed by politicians, yet also apparently backed by near-consensus among scientists – is having, and will continue to have, a decisive effect on the role and output of landscape and garden designers through the early 21st century and beyond. This marks a paradigm shift, or tipping point, for the profession as a whole. There will, of course, be development in the understanding of issues around climate change, sea-level rise, population explosion (leading to ever-expanding cities), water scarcity, fuel shortages and species extinction, but the fundamental idea that landscape design must be seen to be ecologically responsible ('sustainable') is here to stay.

Sustainability is, for many in the design professions, the new imperative – a 'game-changer'. It is relevant, too, to architecture and other disciplines, but since 'ecology' was already more or less within landscape design's perceived realm of expertise, the profession has been experiencing an unprecedented frisson of importance within the design hierarchy. There has also been a change in the scale of work undertaken. Landscape-architecture firms have increasingly branded themselves as 'urban planners' (first and most notably in the Netherlands, where Adriaan Geuze's West 8 led the way), massively enlarging the scope of the work they might have traditionally undertaken.

Despite the 'green' euphoria of the 1990s, the landscape profession was poorly equipped to deal with many of the complex technical challenges presented by the sustainability agenda. Instead, there was a great deal of commercially expedient eco-posturing, as firms tried to make themselves and their work seem relevant in a world where porous paving was suddenly more desirable than Carrara marble. Some attempted to appease the burgeoning eco-bureaucracy by adopting the formal vocabulary of sustainability, perhaps inevitably downplaying aesthetic considerations in the process. Some practices even made sustainability their raison d'être.[1]

The timing of the eco-revolution was not propitious for landscape, since it happened to coincide with a shift in the professional design hierarchy from the 1980s, which saw landscape architecture supplanted in towns and cities by the new doctrines of urbanism. This 'new urbanism' was a largely architecturally driven discipline that quickly established itself at faculty level in universities across America and in parts of Europe. During the 1990s urban designers from architectural backgrounds began to win much of the work previously allotted to landscape architects, only a minority of whom rebranded themselves (or else subdivisions of their companies) in order to assimilate the new categorization. Landscape architecture was now partially supplanted by an urban-design ethos that saw buildings, street furniture and other 'things' privileged above concepts of space and movement. Perhaps landscape architects were too busy grappling with the urgent challenge of the new eco-agenda throughout the 1990s to be able to act coherently. A decade later, landscape architecture woke up and issued a riposte in the form of the doctrine of 'landscape urbanism'.[2]

What is landscape urbanism?

It's difficult to know quite how to define landscape urbanism.[3] It is the buzz-phrase in the American universities, led by Harvard's Graduate School of Design, the Universities of Pennsylvania and Princeton, as well as outposts such as the Architectural Association in London.[4] There have been several conferences, blogs and volumes of essays (including *The Landscape Urbanism Reader*, 2006) dedicated to this 'discipline', and most recently a mammoth tome entitled *Ecological Urbanism* (2010), a kind of eco-rebrand of the original.

Every theorist and designer seems to have a different idea about what landscape urbanism is. While this gives it a genuine value as an invigorating talking shop, on the ground there are not really any places to which one can point and say: 'Look! It's landscape urbanism!' Just three exemplars are regularly cited by landscape urbanists: the (unrealized) 1980s plan for Parc de la Villette, in Paris, by Rem Koolhaas and the Office for Metropolitan Architecture (OMA); the entries of the shortlisted finalists in Toronto's Downsview Park competition (the winner was a design called 'Tree City', by Koolhaas, Bruce Mau and others); and the High Line park in New York, by James Corner of Field Operations, with planting designs from Piet Oudolf (see p. 206). The argument that these three projects can be described as landscape urbanism is based on the assertion that each treats the ground plane in landscape terms first and foremost, essentially privileging the horizontal (landscape) above the vertical (architecture), and the concept of surface above form.[5] They are also seen as 'open-ended' designs that embrace concepts of change and development, in which the 'plan' is less something to be seen on paper as a system that is instigated and then husbanded. These assertions are neither novel nor controversial in the realm of landscape and garden design.

Rem Koolhaas, in his seminal *S, M, L, XL* (1995), was writing about architecture/ urbanism, but his ideas eventually came to be applied fruitfully to landscape architecture and city planning. 'If there is to be a "new urbanism",' he wrote, in Foucauldian mode, 'it will not be based on the twin fantasies of order and omnipotence; it will be the staging of uncertainty; it will no longer be concerned with the arrangement of more or less permanent objects, but with the irrigation of territories with potential; it will no longer aim for stable configurations, but for the creation of enabling fields that accommodate processes that refuse to be crystallized into definitive form; it will no longer be about meticulous definition, the imposition of limits, but about expanding notions, denying boundaries; not about separating and identifying entities, but about discovering unnameable hybrids; it will no longer be obsessed with the city, but with the manipulation of infrastructure for endless intensifications and diversifications, shortcuts and redistributions – the reinvention of psychological space.'[6]

Koolhaas's contribution had the abiding merit of originality (which many in the profession still find difficult to forgive). His use of the city of Atlanta as an exemplar was also to prove inspirational to a new generation: 'Atlanta does not have the classical symptoms of the city; it is not dense; it is a sparse, thin carpet of habitation, a kind of suprematist composition of little fields. Its strongest contextual givens are vegetal and infrastructural: forests and road. Atlanta is not a city; it is a landscape.'[7] This view of the urban fabric, which owes something to Frank Lloyd Wright's unrealized, utopian Broadacre City scheme (founded on a structure of agricultural fields), soon emerged as a key early tenet of landscape urbanism.

From the start, landscape urbanism was a theoretical methodology, a framework for discourse, as opposed to a 'school' of work. Lacking a sense of consistency, landscape urbanism has perhaps been best characterized as a 'design ethic'.[8] Ideas around it have been refined repeatedly, an early example being Alex Wall's summary: 'The term landscape no longer refers to prospects of pastoral innocence, but rather invokes the functioning matrix of connective tissue that organizes not only objects and spaces, but also the dynamic processes and events that move through them. This is the landscape as active surface, structuring the conditions for new relationships and interactions among the things it supports.'[9]

Koolhaas's earlier musings were thus transformed into an even more mysterious prescription for towns and cities, as landscape urbanists struggle to convert their bold ideas into a semblance of physical reality.[10] And like the Modernists before them, they choose to deride a straw man of supposed 'pastoral innocence' – a caricature of the 18th-century English landscape school – as a means of exaggerating the functional efficacy of their own propositions.

Perhaps the closest we have to a standard definition of landscape urbanism today has come from Charles Waldheim, chair of the landscape school at Harvard's Graduate School of Design and, as editor of *The Landscape Urbanism Reader*, its principal cheerleader: 'Landscape urbanism describes a disciplinary realignment currently underway in which the idea of landscape supplants architecture as the basic building block of city-making, especially when contemporary urban conditions are characterized by horizontal sprawl and rapid change. Landscape, under these circumstances, is often able to reproduce urban effects traditionally achieved through the construction of buildings simply through the organization of low and roughly horizontal surfaces.' [11]

The city as metaphor

On one level, landscape urbanism is a straightforward attack on the pre-existing hierarchy of urban design, in which architecture is historically privileged because cities have been seen as agglomerations of buildings. As early as 1994, the influential British architectural critic Kenneth Frampton had come round to this point of view, suggesting: 'We may assert that landscaped form as the fundamental material of a fragmentary urbanism is of greater consequence than the free-standing aestheticized object'. Frampton's migration in the early 1990s – away from a focus on the built environment and towards an understanding of urban fabric as landscape – perhaps presages a trajectory that the architectural profession itself is only now beginning to describe (to the palpable delight of many in the landscape profession). [12]

Landscape urbanism is sustained by metaphor. One of its core ideas is that a city can be looked upon as either a machine-like system, or an organism or ecosystem that is self-sustaining and self-directing: an urban metabolism. The 'city as machine' idea is an old chestnut of Corbusian Modernism, and fails to take into account the massive emotional impact of the contemporary ecological crisis, which means that ideas of 'nature' are more privileged than other constituent elements of the system. The idea of the 'city as organism' has become much more attractive as a result of the sustainability agenda, and the notion is often dropped (unexamined) into discussions of landscape urbanism. Alan Berger, in his essay 'Drosscape' in *The Landscape Urbanism Reader*, posits this at one extreme: 'Cities are not static objects, but active arenas marked by continuous energy flows and transformations of which landscapes and buildings and other hard parts are not permanent structures but transitional manifestations. Like a biological organism, the urbanized landscape is an open system'.[13]

Arising from this kind of thinking is a convenient fantasy that underpins landscape urbanism: the notion that the growth of towns and cities is somehow inevitable and intractable, with design acting as, at best, a mediating agent or salve. Cities, however, are not self-sustaining organisms. Urban areas can be planned, designed and regulated like any other civic construct, if the will is there. Additionally, American cities are not fundamentally different to cities in other parts of the world, in terms of their function and the requirements of the populace: the construction of a myth of American urban and suburban exceptionalism must be resisted. The highway-dominated outskirts and multiple faceless suburbs of so many American cities are not products of topography, climate or blind fate, but have sprung from a financially and aesthetically deregulated culture, an extremity of market-driven capitalism that has led to a debased geography, which must now be navigated somehow by its beleaguered citizens, chained to their cars and prescribed road routes.

In fact, cities were designed (or rather not designed) by human beings, and as a result turned into these alienated zones dominated by arterial roads, advertising hoardings, empty lots, car parks, identikit malls and meaningless miniature suburbs.

Sprawl. It was partly the mainstream design profession itself – aesthetically supine, commercially driven – that created this situation, in most cases acting alongside a vacuum where planning regulation should have been. To imply that this chaos is some kind of natural evolution in the life of cities is to sidestep culpability – not just on the part of designers and local authorities, but on the part of humanity in general.[14]

And yet, while professing relative helplessness in the face of the city as organism, landscape urbanists also like to pose as heroic interventionists, suggesting they roll out some 'system' that is somehow expected to heal ecological, social, economic and political scars.[15] There is a comparison to be made here with Victorian paternalism. The parks movement from the mid-19th century onwards in England, subsequently exported to the USA (courtesy of Frederick Law Olmsted) and elsewhere, equated an orderly and well-maintained public realm with an orderly and well-maintained populace. The sustainability agenda has also led to the idea that landscape design should actively promote good health, both physical and moral. The Victorian city fathers surmised that their only motivation was improving people's lives, but it was also in part about consolidating their own professional and social status, controlling the populace, and creating a lasting memorial to themselves and their enlightened era. Landscape urbanists also subscribe to this idea, but with less public good to show for it. Victorian parks creators had a strictly bounded sense of the extent of their own influence, whereas today's landscape urbanists see the entire town or city as their potential canvas, with every square millimetre subject to their design sensibility. Cities have historically been centres of dissent and transgressive behaviour. Landscape urbanism threatens to turn them into totems of political expediency and ecological correctness.[16]

Perhaps it is not necessary, after all, for every landscape architect to formulate a personal philosophy of the cosmos and start designing whole cities. Doing a good job at ground level is pretty important, too. Rather than attempting to devise some kind of overarching, utopian 'system' that will unite entire cities, landscape architects might profitably concentrate instead on short, sharp, intense interventions at key interstices of the urban environment. Public parks, plazas and squares remain the most important landscape interventions that designers can make, and those teaching the next generation of landscape architects would do well to acknowledge this.

1 Panayiota Pyla observed a comparable movement in architecture during this period: 'The concept of sustainability gave architecture a new purpose. According to this point of view, sustainability emerged not a moment too soon, just when the profession's search for meaning (e.g. historicist trends of the late 20th century) or the egocentrism of the signature designer (e.g., the legacy of Modernism) had led to dead ends.' 'Counter-Histories of Sustainability', in *Volume* 18 (2008).

2 'I coined the term "landscape urbanism" in 1996 based on conversations with James Corner on the notion of "landscape as urbanism". This neologism formed the basis of a conference at the Graham Foundation in Chicago (1997) and new academic programs in the schools of architecture at the University of Chicago and the Architectural Association, London.' Charles Waldheim, 'Precedents for a North American Landscape Urbanism', in *Center 14: On Landscape Urbanism*, ed. Dean Almy (Austin: The Center for American Architecture and Design, University of Texas at Austin, 2007): 303.

3 Urbanism, new urbanism, landscape urbanism, sustainable urbanism and now ecological urbanism are all about a profession, or a group of professions, attempting to redefine themselves.

4 Backed by powerful American universities with faculties packed with 'guest-lecturer' designers, the doctrine of landscape urbanism is difficult to gainsay, professionally speaking (for example, all fourteen contributors to *The Landscape Urbanism Reader* are lecturers and professors within university departments, as well as being practitioners in most cases). As a result, there is little dissent.

5 Some commentators, such as Stan Allen, have sought to strip landscape design down to its basics in order to find a starting point for landscape urbanism: 'Infrastructure works not so much to propose specific buildings on given sites, but to construct the site itself. Infrastructure prepares the ground for future building and relates the conditions for future events. Its primary modes of operation are: the division, allocation and construction of surfaces; the provision of services to support future programs; and the establishment of networks for movement, communication and exchange. Infrastructure's medium is geography.' He goes on to suggest that infrastructures are 'flexible and anticipatory'. 'Infrastructural Urbanism', in Almy, 179. Landscape ecologist Richard T. T. Forman, on the other hand, lists seventy-five different kinds of green space to be found in urban and suburban areas in *Urban Regions: Ecology and Planning Beyond the City* (Cambridge, England: Cambridge University Press, 2008).

6 'Whatever Happened to Urbanism', in Rem Koolhaas and Bruce Mau, *S, M, L, XL* (New York: Monacelli Press, 1995): 965.

7 *The Landscape Urbanism Reader*, ed. Charles Waldheim (New York: Princeton Architectural Press, 2006): 43.

8 James Corner has described this as 'layering'. (Almy, 163).

9 Alex Wall, 'Programming the Urban Surface', in *Recovering Landscape: Essays in Contemporary Landscape Theory*, ed. James Corner (New York: Princeton Architectural Press, 2000).

10 What Richard Weller dubs 'a fuzzy cluster of rhetorical positioning [that is] largely unsubstantiated by work on the ground'. (Waldheim, 71).

11 Almy, 293.

12 The journalistic critic Edwin Heathcote put it most pithily: 'What is extraordinary is how little has been learnt [from the fate of architectural Modernism]. Architects are still conceiving their buildings as monuments; as foreground, not background. The result is a mess.' 'The Regeneration Game', in *The Financial Times*, December 13, 2010.

13 Waldheim, 199.

14 The success of landscape urbanism in North America is linked to the relative lack of high-quality historic environments. In Europe, talk of landscape urbanism must be couched in a historical frame or it is meaningless. The American mode of thinking is to decry the development of cities, or the destruction of the provincial city type, and then indulge in the brutal conceit of 'starting afresh' or 'wiping the slate clean'.

15 As Elizabeth Mossop usefully put it, 'If we think of landscape as an infrastructure that underlies other urban systems, rather than equating it with nature or ecology, we have a much more workable conceptual framework for designing urban systems.' (Waldheim, 176). The problem with this stance today is that it fails to take into account the massive emotional impact of the contemporary ecological crisis.

16 This is perhaps partly borne of the fact that landscape urbanism is basically about retro-fitting or remodelling (or 'recovering', to use James Corner's more emotive term), as opposed to creating something visionary and new.

FORMWERKZ

SINGAPORE

Progressive architects who have begun to design truly 'inside-outside' private houses that incorporate garden areas into the built fabric.

This Singapore-based company was founded in 1998 by Alan Tay, Berlin Lee and Seetoh Kum Loon, with Gwen Tan joining as fourth partner in 2002. Now numbering about twenty staff, the office's collaborative atmosphere allows it to offer expertise across architecture, urban, interior and landscape design. Many firms claim to cover all these disciplines, but very few demonstrate a relatively equal distribution between them. A number of houses designed by the firm have substantial designed garden spaces that are integral to the design as a whole. Formwerkz states: 'We have no interest in architecture that is preoccupied with an obsessive pursuit of minimal refinement. Rather, we want our efforts to be directed towards the recovery of mutual human relationships, and the restoration of primordial relationships between man and nature. We are keen to design happenings – or more precisely, conditions – that can espouse more active engagement between man and his environment.'

The Origami House (2010), in Singapore, was designed for a family of three. The private spaces are enclosed in a 'sculptural loop', which is poised above the living areas and kitchen on the ground floor, with a swimming pool outside. The swimming pool is lined with a mosaic of tiles featuring pixellated blossoms. Fringed with palms, ferns and other subtropical flora, it provides an opportunity to introduce a sense of the garden invading the interior spaces at lower levels. In the basement is a multi-entertainment area and another (ornamental) pool. The folding planes of the house, notably its rooflines and terraces or balconies, gave rise to the 'origami' metaphor. The result is that the interior spaces offer a multiplicity of different, 'non-standard' volumes, while the balconies provide opportunities for verdant planting.

01 The basement-level pool at the Origami House in Singapore, where a vertical garden links indoor with outdoor. The bulging wooden structure on the right is the staircase.

02 One of the spaces decorated with plants
   is the shuttered bathroom.
03 The section illustrates how the interior
   and exterior spaces of the Origami House
   are folded into each other, as a result of
   the novel architectural approach.
04 The swimming pool is decorated with tiles
   that depict pixellated blossoms.

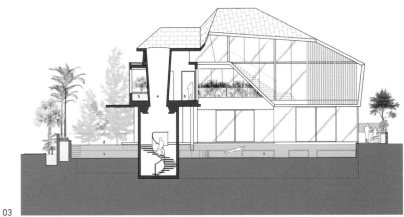

02

03

06

07

05-07 At the Maximum Garden House, Formwerkz
conjured garden elements and spaces out
of a building plot whose footprint had to be
almost entirely taken up by the house itself.
The front elevation features a green wall,
while the sloping roof of the house becomes
a viewing and sunbathing deck.
08 The 'family hall' is a permeable space,
where the maximum amount of greenery
is encouraged to permeate.
09 A detail of the shuttering of the green wall
on the front of the house: it allows air in and
keeps rain out.

The plan for the Maximum Garden House (2010), in Jalam Rendang, Singapore, grew out of a frustration with the idea that when a client has bought a piece of real estate, the entire plot should always be used for the building. Formwerkz felt that owners should have the 'maximum' amount of garden space possible at their property: 'Outdoor spaces are essential for one's connection with the land, or at least the perception of living in a landed property, as opposed to living in a high-rise condominium. Our key strategy was to seek out and reclaim incidental spaces or surfaces of the building envelope. The main areas we looked into included the front boundary wall, the car porch and apron roof, the façade and the main house roof. If these incidental spaces or surfaces could be reclaimed, we would potentially gain back 100 per cent of the outdoor space lost to the building.'

The most striking aspect to the front elevation of the house is its 'planter façade': a permeable curtain wall made of living material, adjacent to the main bedroom. Directly below this, on the garage roof, is a planting scheme of amorphous shapes that was inspired by the work of the great Brazilian garden designer, Roberto Burle Marx. A niche in the front wall of the property, adjacent to the street, has been made into a green wall – another statement of intent. The most surprising element of the design is the dramatically sloping roof/deck, which is reached by a ramp from the upper, main-bedroom level. Formwerkz intended this space to become a spot for lying down, as if in a park, chatting or just enjoying the view of the neighbourhood from a high vantage point.

08

09

GREENINC

JOHANNESBURG, SOUTH AFRICA

Confident design team that integrates an African
sensibility and aesthetic into all its work.

Founded in 1995 by Anton Comrie and Stuart Glen, GREENinc has in recent years
secured commissions for some of South Africa's most high-profile projects, including
the Freedom Park in Pretoria and the University of Johannesburg Arts Centre. The
company instinctively associates its landscape designs with the natural environment,
in much the same way that Australian designers remain in thrall to their own astound-
ing landscape. But GREENinc must also be politically astute, framing its statements
and the direction of its output to reflect the country's recent political turmoil and
potential for recovery and development.

The Freedom Park (2011), a joint-venture project by the Newtown Bagale
GREENinc Momo (NBGM) team, mandated by Nelson Mandela as the natural outcome
of the Truth and Reconciliation Commission, acts as a garden of remembrance and
healing. Five narrative episodes are embedded in the design, of which the most important is the *S'khumbuto* memorial, in the heart of the park. Here, a stone building – the
Sanctuary – provides the backdrop to an amphitheatre, which is formed of grassed
terraces and terminates in a wild olive tree planted by Thabo Mbeki in 2002. Sweeping
down from the tree are succulent plants, indigenous aloes and veldt grasses, which
create a visual link to the ridge beyond. Water has been used extensively across the site
because of its relationship to healing and importance in African traditional culture. A
line of encircling 'reeds' (actually, stainless-steel rods) was introduced to symbolize
communication between heaven and earth. There are a number of other distinct areas
in the park that visitors experience in order, including the *Moshate* (a Sotho word
meaning 'the chief's residence'), a 'forest' of majestic *Aloe marlothii*, and, lower down,

01 The *Mveledzo*, or 'path of contemplation', in the Freedom Park, which winds round the hilltop.

02 A 'forest' of *Aloe marlothii* marks the entrance to the *Moshate* (chief's residence) at the western edge of the amphitheatre.
03 The *S'khumbuto*, or memorial space, at the heart of the park, where the Sanctuary is the focus of the amphitheatre.
04 The metal 'reeds' that encircle the amphitheatre can be seen from miles away, and are a reference to an important African belief that reeds serve as conduits between heaven and earth.

the swirling *Uitspanplek* (an Afrikaans word for resting place), representing a deliberate break with the design narrative of the rest of the site.

At the University of Johannesburg's Arts Centre (2006), the main landscape space – the 'green bowl' – had to function as an arrival space and spill-out area for theatregoers during intermissions. This is facilitated by a panel of concrete paving that extends from the lobby into the lawn, while the directional flow away from the building is emphasized by inlaid granite strips, a monolithic concrete bench and a water feature. A relatively narrow concrete staircase mounts the embankment towards the main entrance; this sole angled element is reconciled with the Arts Centre's strong lines by a contrasting serpentine timber walk, the only curved element. The embankment was sculpted into a series of terraces in a nod to the concentric circles of the main campus's landscaped courtyard. The planting in this space was limited to an evergreen lawn to keep the view towards the main buildings open, and to complement the minimalist architecture. At the opening ceremony for the Arts Centre, the lawn was 'branded' by artist Strijdom van der Merwe. The intention was that this installation would be allowed to grow over and disappear, but it is so well loved that it has been maintained as part of the landscape. The zero-depth water feature was designed in collaboration with artist Marco Cianfanelli, and boasts cast-concrete relief work and laser-cut stainless-steel elements. Water enters via hidden nozzles in the finely stepped relief forms, gradually filling up and emptying again in a slow cycle. The ever-changing mood of the feature is further punctuated by sprays from numerous small jets that lend it a playful and celebratory air. Various text inscriptions add another

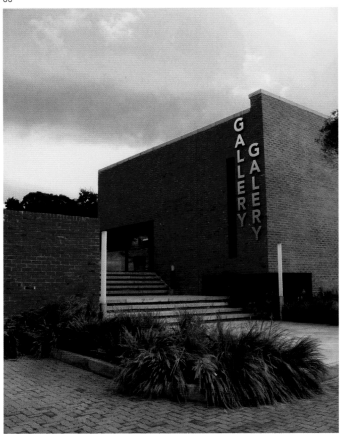

level of meaning to the landscape; poems in local languages were inscribed onto the granite strips worked into the paving in front of the theatre.

The Forum Homini project (2006) was a landscape for a new boutique hotel in a private game reserve near the Sterkfontein Caves. GREENinc reinstated the indigenous high-veld landscape up to the edges and over the rooftops of the buildings so that they appear to emerge from the ground. Sandstone pillars, carved by artist Dave Rossouw, entice guests down a ramp into the heart of the complex. At the base of the ramp, the reception area, restaurant, library and conference facility are arranged around a lower courtyard and a higher, landscaped terrace. The courtyard symbolizes the 'hard' times of mankind's evolutionary path, with concrete paving, sandstone seating, gravel and wild olive trees. The lush planting of the upper terrace is an expression of the 'good' times of man's existence; many of the plant species were chosen because they played a culinary or utilitarian role in the lives of the primitive people that resided here. A low electric fence intended to discourage hippos from entering the grounds did little to deter antelope from grazing on the 'cultivated' landscape, so GREENinc planted sour, less palatable grass species in the veldgrass mixes. The antelope, however, continue to make use of the hotel's swimming pool.

05-09 The main landscape feature at the University of Johannesburg's new Arts Centre is a 'green bowl' of stepped turf embankments. Visitors are encouraged out into the space by a series of directional paths and paved areas, as well as a striking water feature by Marco Cianfanelli and a 'branded' lawn.

07

08

09

10 At the Forum Homini Hotel, the design
   team collaborated with the architects to
   create the sense that the guest pavilions
   were embedded into the ancient landscape,
   known as the 'Cradle of Humankind' due to
   the many fossils of early hominids that have
   been found there.

11 A sculpture by Marco Cianfanelli entitled
   The Sum of Us marks the entrance to the
   hotel. Each layer of steel is an expression of
   a critical stage in the evolution of man.

10

11

JUAN GRIMM

SANTIAGO, CHILE

Thoroughgoing knowledge of the natural flora enables this
experienced designer to create glamorous spaces in keeping
with the natural surroundings.

Over a long career (he has completed more than 350 commissions), Juan Grimm has
specialized in naturalistic gardens of mainly native plants that complement both the
clean lines of modern architecture and the magnificence of Chile's natural surroundings. His simple yet strong philosophy of landscape gardening is based on ecology
before aesthetics; Grimm strongly believes in allowing the existing or underlying
landscape to sing out in any domestic garden setting. The key to his planting style is
the way the shapes of the plant drifts seem to enhance the shape of the land. The
designer also points out that the very act of placing a house in the landscape changes
the conditions for plants – creating shade where there was none before, for example.

The Chapel Garden project (1998), located within Roble Park, in Concepción,
Chile, was part of a programme that saw the gradual development of a holiday village
in a former timber plantation. All of the buildings in the complex, apart from the
glass-walled chapel, are traditional in style. The siting of the chapel was important: an
existing acacia forest was retained because its protecting shade and quietness were felt
to be conducive to prayer. The garden design pays tribute to this sense of seclusion
and simplicity, with its variety of ferns, mosses and other predominantly green plants,
including *Lophosoria quadripinnata*, *Gunnera tinctoria*, *Libertia chilensis*, *Blechnum
chilensis*, *Drimys winteri*, boxwood, *Vinca minor* and hebe and choysia species.

At Bahía Azul, also in Chile, Grimm's own holiday home (1990 to present) sits
on the edge of the rocky cliffs overlooking the Pacific Ocean. His main design objec-
tive was to ensure that the house's volume became an integral part of the hills and
rocks, making the garden a link between the architecture and the natural landscape.

02

03

01 The Chapel Garden consists of mainly green, shade-loving plants, which are intended to enhance the tranquil atmosphere within the Modernist chapel.

02-04 Grimm's own holiday home at Bahía Azul overlooks the Pacific Ocean, a vantage point chosen for its views. The idea behind the design of the house and garden was to create a property that appears at one with the site.

04

08
09

05-09 The circular swimming pool is designed
so that bathers cannot see the ocean, but
can hear it. A long staircase hewn in the
rock creates a dramatic entry for visitors
descending from the car parking area
above. Throughout, Grimm has aimed for
a felicitous balance between architecture
and native plants.

Grimm identifies three specific intermediate spaces. The first is between the car park
and the access to the house, and was planted with exotic vegetation with the sole aim
of providing protection to native plants. The second space is between the building's
southwest exit towards the garden, where a sheltered courtyard becomes an anteroom
between house and garden. The third space, housing the swimming pool, is sheltered
by rocks from the southern winds. Native species such as baccharis, alstroemeria,
orchids, cacti and succulents were planted on top of the rocks that surround the pool
to suggest that they had always existed there. Over the years, vines have begun to grow
over the exterior walls. The relationship between house and vegetation is intended to
echo that which exists between the rocks and shrubs that spontaneously develop along
the shoreline and up the cliffs. Among the decorative species planted around the
building are *Schinus latifolius*, *Maytenus boaria*, *Escallonia pulverulenta*, *Baccharis
concave*, *Baccharis linearis*, *Lobelia tupa*, *Puya venusta*, *Puya chilensis*, *Cupressus
macrocarpa* and *Myoporum laetum*.

An enthusiasm for native plants and for naturalistic design is now a worldwide
phenomenon, of course, but few practitioners are as devoted to replicating the forms
of natural flora as Grimm. Such replication makes for a garden style with less immedi-
ate decorative appeal, perhaps, but at the same time it can imbue a manmade landscape with something of the integrity of nature in the raw, and also act as a celebration
of the way that plant communities create their own subtle but insistent rhythms
in the wild.

HAGER

ZÜRICH, SWITZERLAND

Innovative landscape design that effortlessly
straddles the garden/landscape divide.

Guido Hager has worked as an independent landscape architect since 1984. In 2000 he formed Hager Landschaftsarchitektur with Patrick Altermatt, and in 2007 established Hager International in collaboration with Pascal Posset. Both firms currently employ thirty-five members of staff. Like Fernando Caruncho (see p. 38), Hager likes to frame his work in terms of the classical world; in his case, through evocation of a golden age when man lived in absolute harmony with nature. Hager posits landscape design as an attempt to glimpse once again something of that paradisical realm.

One of the most dramatic and unlikely settings for such a foray into paradise reinvented is a derelict 1950s petrol station, located in the densely built-up Schönberg area of Berlin (2008). The new owner wanted to transform the site into a private residence, but had to convince the authorities that the building, when thoroughly renovated and supplemented by a glass studio in a walled garden, was exactly the right solution for this exposed location. The client envisioned a garden based around the 'Three Friends in Winter': pine, whose crown protectively bears the snow; bamboo, whose evergreen appearance embodies eternal life; and the ornamental cherry, the first tree to begin blooming while it is still winter. Hager was inspired, he says, 'by a film, *Giulietta degli spiriti* by Federico Fellini, and its atmosphere – the heat of the summer, the fragrance of the stone pine, the chirping of crickets'. The large pine *Pinus sylvestris*, along with the multiple-trunk ornamental cherry tree *Prunus x yedoensis*, form the framework of trees. Three types of bamboo behind 2m- (6 ft 6 in-) high walls shield the residence from the street and the neighbouring properties. The central area is covered with gravel, with islands of perennials supplemented by aquilegia,

01 A 1950s garage forecourt in central Berlin was transformed into the front garden of a sleek and glamorous new residence, complete with an ornamental pool and self-seeding perennials.

03

04

02-04 A heady, escapist Mediterranean dream garden was inserted into the delightful retro-styling of the old petrol station.

willow-leafed sunflower, *Gaura lindheimeri* and Jerusalem sage. It is intended that the gravel area will become overgrown with self-seeding perennials. Under the roof above the petrol pumps, fish can be seen in the 18m- (59 ft-) long, 2.5m- (8 ft-) wide water channel, as they snap at mosquitoes amid yellow iris and water lilies.

In Vienna, Hager created a new park for a new district. Rudolf-Bednar-Park (2008) was constructed on the site of an old train station, and the course of the railway lines was incorporated into the groundplan. The park re-opens up this part of the city to the Danube River, with a variety of different spaces or episodes, from high-density sports fields to horticulturally intense areas. The Quartiersgarten is the most ambitious: a geometrically organized space with fragmented beds, carefully colour-themed, and wide paths between them. At the southwestern edge, towards the site of a proposed school, lies a sports zone with a skating facility, courts and pitches.

The northeastern area, near residential buildings on the Vorgartenstraße, is reserved for calmer pursuits, such as games of bocce or picnics, as well as play options for children, marked by orange-coloured poles that have been used to designate a range of play elements, including climbing frames, swings and large, communal hammocks. The central spaces of the park are defined by broad expanses of lawn. The Schilfgarten (reed gardens) traverse the park between the lawn areas. As a reference to the landscape space of the river, these flat pools of water planted with reeds offer a place for retreat and contemplation, and are lit at night during the evening hours when the park remains open.

05-06 The Rudolf-Bednar-Park's Quartiersgarten, with its distinctive plan and colour-theming, offers a verdant and decorative alternative to the kinds of frenetic activity that occurs elsewhere in the park.

07 The park's groundplan retains certain elements of the train station it replaces, including sections of old railway line.

08-09 A convention of bright-orange poles clearly mark out areas and features that have been designed for sport or play.

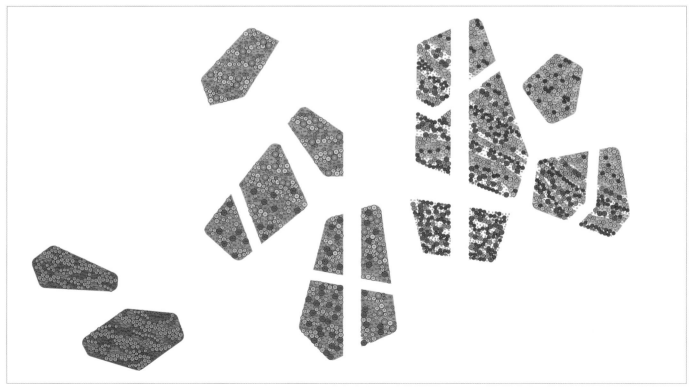

07

08

09

HOCKER DESIGN GROUP

DALLAS, TEXAS, USA

A recently established company rapidly reaching its creative potential, with a string of award-winning projects.

David L. Hocker founded his company in 2005, and employs just two other landscape architects. The tiny scale of his operation, however, has not prevented the firm from winning a string of awards, including two American Society of Landscape Architecture Honor Awards in 2010. Hocker's particular horticultural interest is in indigenous plants, especially those from his native Texas, where he also trained in landscape architecture. Two semesters spent in Italy during his training made a strong impression; his philosophy is 'design is in the details'.

The Kessler residence (2009), in Dallas, is a glass box of a house that sits commandingly on a wooded limestone hill, and presented a challenge in the creation of usable outdoor space. There was also the opportunity to create a small, intimate courtyard in an unused void beneath the soaring structure. A stone bridge takes visitors to the buildings that constitute the residence, where a steep incline between the street and the house suggested the creation of a garden. Winding concrete steps begin the journey up the terrain to the house, where masses of Turk's cap flank the steps. A custom-designed gabion wall retains earth from the adjacent property, and serves as an extension of the main building. A linear pond below this wall lies parallel to the house, and abuts a floor-to-ceiling glass wall, allowing the water feature to be seen from both the outdoor lounge and inside the house. Crushed green aggregate and oversized flagstones provide the flooring for the exterior lounge, a material that crosses over the pond to the front door. A canopy extends from the house to cover the lounge, which seems tucked between architecture and landscape. Stairs link to the back of the property, creating a sloped garden of native plants between the two buildings.

01 At the Kessler residence, in Dallas, a garden with pool was formed out of an apparently redundant area of land in a steep dip between the house and the road. A thicket of native planting surrounds the glass house, which also features a fish pool crossed by a simple, concrete-slab bridge.

03

04

02-04 The cool outdoor lounge area in the Kessler's residence's courtyard space is secreted away beneath a building that is next to an extension to the fish pool.

At the Midbury House, also in Dallas, a small entry garden forms a platform for displaying native plants. Horizontal concrete bands lead from a small grass paver plinth, while elevated steel planters, filled with monocultural plantings of Texas sage, prickly pear and gulf muhly grass, rise up from a verdant carpet of turf. Near the house, a stucco wall terminates in a galvanized pipe that spills water into a concrete trough below, creating a soothing soundscape. The garden was designed with both low maintenance and low water-use in mind.

Yet another project in the city is the Power House, a 0.2-hectare (0.5-acre) landscape around a redundant electricity substation that dates back to 1923, now reconfigured as a single-family residence. Hocker preserved the integrity of the original external groundplan, although the transformers and other electrical equipment are long gone. In the inner courtyard, a rising plinth with rusted Corten steel sides contains a simple, rectangular lawn of buffalo grass. A lone mesquite tree creates shadows on the basalt gravel, and the surrounding high brick walls add to the sense of drama, while providing a sense of privacy. On another elevation, panels of wildflowers create a postindustrial frisson.

08

10

09

05-07 The entrance courtyard at the Midbury
House, in Dallas, where Hocker introduced
elevated rusted-steel planters that contain
single species.

08-10 Hocker created a landscape design for
a redundant electricity substation (now
a private residence), which incorporates
panels of turf and wildflowers, and a rising
grass berm.

HOERR SCHAUDT

CHICAGO, ILLINOIS, USA

A large company specializing in corporate and commercial work, injecting potentially dull schemes with vision and life.

Having successfully practised as individuals for several decades, landscape architects Doug Hoerr and Peter Lindsay Schaudt joined forces as Hoerr Schaudt in 2008, with some forty employees on staff. They have designed a string of large-scale and high-profile public commissions and have gained numerous plaudits, while maintaining a practice that also caters for private residential commissions.

The Gary Comer Youth Center (2008), named for a local entrepreneur and philanthropist, is located on an infill site in the disadvantaged South Side neighbourhood of Chicago. Since the centre is close to a railway and surrounded by a main road and parking, with little access to safe outdoor environments, Hoerr Schaudt was asked to install a community vegetable and fruit garden (760m², or 8,181 sq ft) as a form of green roof, to be used primarily by local children and senior citizens. Soil at 46cm (18 in) to 61cm (24 in) deep allows for the cultivation of crops, including cabbage, sunflowers, carrots, lettuce, potatoes and strawberries. Sharp differences between temperatures on the ground and those on the roof mean that the rooftop is effectively in a different climate zone, and can be utilized as a growing space throughout the winter. The garden is surrounded by the third-floor classrooms and circulation corridor; as students move from one classroom to another, floor-to-ceiling windows transform this working garden into a viewable space. Plastic lumber made from recycled milk containers forms pathways that align with the courtyard's window frames, while metal circles scattered throughout the garden serve as elements of artistic expression and function as skylights, illuminating the gymnasium and café below.

01

02

01-02 The rooftop vegetable garden at the
Gary Comer Youth Center in Chicago is
visually connected with the top-floor
classrooms, which look directly onto it.
The circular objects are skylights.

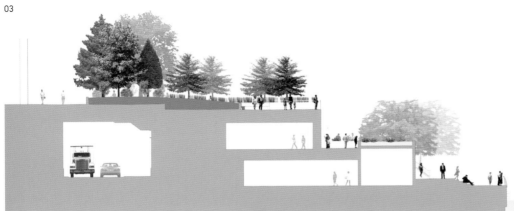

03 The garden at the Trump International Hotel and Tower in Chicago has been created over three tiers, descending to the riverside walkway, in contrast to the surrounding architecture.
04 The garden is entirely composed of native plants from the local area.
05 The tripartite groundplan, linking the hotel and tower to the riverside, can be appreciated in plan from the top of the building.
06–08 The juxtaposition of Modernist architecture with native plants is the keynote idea of this design.

Hoerr Schaudt's design for the upper plaza of the Trump International Hotel and Tower (2009), also in Chicago, features nearly 1,500m² (16,146 sq ft) of native plants commonly found along Illinois's riverbanks. It is the first native-plant landscape for a major commercial building in the downtown area. The unusual planting palette highlights the original ecology of the project's riverfront location, and is a stark contrast to the sleek façade of the structure. Though technically the second-tallest building in the city, the tower, located on the Chicago River in the heart of the 'Loop', occupies a prominent position in the city's skyline. In spite of its size, the building has a relatively slim footprint, allowing for significant open space. The dense mix of finely textured native plants, including horsetail, Joe-Pye weed, alders and bottlebrush buckeye (*Aesculus parviflora*), rise from plant beds that have been elevated to balance the height of the architecture and to provide seating. Approximately 65 per cent of the species are native, and the remaining 35 per cent were selected to help increase the plant diversity and long-term viability of the site, and are well adapted to the region. Curved pathways draw visitors from the upper garden to the river via a terraced stair, designed to draw attention to the water below. Three tiers break up the descent to the city's public riverside walkway, and seating along the way encourages people to pause and enjoy views of the river and facing skyline.

06

07

08

HOOD DESIGN

Well-established practice that continues to push the
boundaries between landscape, architecture, urban design,
environmentalism and city planning.

Walter Hood established Hood Design Studio in 1992, and from the beginning the
firm has concentrated its efforts in the public realm, addressing the reconstruction of
urban landscapes within towns and cities. The studio has been one of the pioneers of
a practical design method that is founded squarely on research, in conjunction with
aesthetics and ecological concerns. As is often the case in the profession, this is an
attitude that many landscape firms claim as integral to their approach, but few follow
through conclusively. The company strives 'to develop new elements, spatial forms
and objects that validate their existing familiar context,' Hood says. 'Project research
includes archival and oral histories, physical, environmental and social patterns and
practices, to uncover familiar and untold stories. These elements are layered together
through an idiosyncratic improvisational design process, which yields familiar yet
new spaces, forms and elements.'

Hood's design for the new M. H. de Young Memorial Museum (2005), in San
Francisco's Golden Gate Park, was conceived as 'an integration of the urban and the
constructed natural landscape', and 'as an interaction between art and park'. Perhaps
the current fashion for ecologically slanted landscape design has influenced the studio's description of its own work, because in the end the landscape surrounding this
museum is a highly artificial, clearly manmade confection, which is crammed with
stimulating artefacts and artistic features (and is no worse for that). This is a complex
series of interlocked spaces, founded on the central idea of grass berms and mounds
that echo the sand-dune typology. In the entry court, Greenmoor stone paving sets
the stage for the sculptor Andy Goldsworthy's *Drawn Line*, a series of boulders marked

01 At the new De Young Museum in San Francisco, the design was based on the natural typology of sand dunes, here transformed into berms and mounds that delineate the different parts of a complex and intense landscape design.

02 The Garden of Enchantment includes water tricks and games familiar from the vocabulary of public landscape design.

03 Even minimalist landscape interventions can become stimulating play environments for imaginative children.

04 This installation by Andy Goldsworthy is a single fissure that can be traced across the ground terrace and through the boulders in the museum's entrance courtyard.

04

05

06

07

05-07 Outdoor installations at the Oakland
Museum: Garden Sculpture (figures 05 and
07) celebrates motifs from the Alhambra
and the Katsura Imperial Palace, while
Canned Spinach (figure 06) was a temporary
installation that consisted of spinach plantings
in reference to the city's canning industry.

by a fissure that can be traced along a single line. This is without doubt the highlight of the exterior landscape. By way of contrast, Hood used simple landscape materials of lawn, limestone and palm trees for the building's frontage. The Garden of Enchantment is a space designed to stimulate movement and inspire children through its playful forms and landscape elements; adjacent is the redesigned, circular Pool of Enchantment. In the Sculpture Garden, a sloping lawn and orthogonal path system create 'rooms' for sculpture and rest. Landforms and plantings blur the edges of the scheme, while the Japanese Tea Garden leads to a sequential set of spaces that eventually reveal artist James Turrell's *Three Jims* skyspace.

At the Oakland Museum (2010), the firm was commissioned to create two installations to mark the museum's new entry point at Oak Street. Canned Spinach was a temporary work that celebrated the city as a historical centre for vegetable and fruit canning (Del Monte was established here in 1916). A mono-crop of spinach was grown in a field of galvanized cans, and was then harvested throughout the summer. During this period, the newly renovated café featured spinach dishes, while visitors were also encouraged to help with the harvest. The other (permanent) artwork, Garden Sculpture, made reference to two great historic gardens: the Alhambra in Spain, and the Katsura Imperial Palace Gardens in Japan. The Alhambra fountain and the Katsura lantern were appropriated and transformed into serialized hanging objects for both the interior and exterior of the museum. The installation, says Hood, was 'placed within occupiable outdoor vitrines, to suggest a space for art that is an experiential zone viewed from within as well as from without'.

CHARLES JENCKS

LONDON, ENGLAND

Pioneer of the use of landform or turf sculpture on a massive scale,
now inflected with archaeological as well as cosmological ideas.

The historian and landscape designer Charles Jencks, celebrated for his early recognition and definition of Postmodernism, has since 1990 also been absorbed by the potential of landscape design to reflect and celebrate contemporary cosmological theory. The principal means by which he does this is through landforming, an aspect of landscape design – frequently religious or ritualistic – that can be traced in various forms through most of the major civilizations, which he has managed to re-imagine in a startlingly contemporary manner (see The Resurgence of Landform; p. 184).

At Jupiter Artland, a new sculpture park created in the landscape surrounding Bonnington House, near Edinburgh, Jencks created a typically arresting piece entitled Life Mounds (2009). Eight landforms and a connecting causeway surround four lakes, creating a positively extraterrestrial vision of sculpted turf terraces and elegant pools of still water, bisected by the entrance drive. For the unsuspecting visitor, this opening artistic salvo is truly startling; it has caused several drivers to veer off the road in shocked delight. It is a great *coup de théâtre du jardin*, which immediately catapults visitors into the spirit of the park. Most will come back to enjoy the piece on foot, for these terraces are designed to be walked up, over and around. As with similar works by Jencks, Life Mounds is 'content-driven' (Jencks's favourite term). In this case, it acts as a symbolic demonstration of the wonders of cell division – the beginning of life itself. As Jencks explains: 'The theme is the life of the cell, cells as the basic units of life, and the way one cell divides into two in stages called "mitosis" (presented in a red sandstone rill). Curving concrete seats have cell models surrounded by Liesegang rocks. Their red iron concentric circles bear an uncanny relationship to the many

01-04 Life Mounds at the Jupiter Artland
sculpture garden, in the grounds of
Bonnington House, near Edinburgh, is a
celebration of the cell as the basis of all
life. The earthwork spirals, pools and other
decorative elements conspire to tell the
'story' of cell division. On arrival, visitors
to the park drive through the middle
of the piece.

organelles inside the units of life. From above, the layout presents their early division into membranes and nuclei, a landform celebration of the cell as the basis of life.' A flat parterre provides a platform for sculpture exhibits.

Jencks's earliest and most celebrated foray into this methodology was the Garden of Cosmic Speculation, located at his own property near Dumfries, Scotland. His late wife Maggie Keswick, the author of a standard work on Chinese gardens, wished to create a sense of the 'bones of the earth' – in this case, gentle downland shaped by a glacier. This was achieved by moving earth to emphasize the natural undulations of parkland to the northwest of the site's Georgian house. The bulldozers were brought in again to make a series of ponds out of an unused marshy area below and to the northeast of the house. The subject of the garden is nothing less than the story of the expanding universe. Jencks describes it as 'a drama of increasing complexity... as unpredictably creative as a mad, 19th-century professor'. There are two principal design motifs: the wave, which warps and folds in on itself, creating a dynamic tension of alternating opposites; and the twist, a symbol of coherent energy. The straight lines of the Platonic tradition are eschewed. A 122m- (400 ft-) long, S-shaped earthwork wave twists sinuously round a smooth pond, warping away from it in terraces to embrace another, much smaller arc of a pond on the other side.

'Garden art is close to autobiography,' Jencks says, 'because it takes years to achieve and the events of one's life get wrapped into its meaning.' To those of us used to seeing his landforms and kinetic sculptures explained solely in terms of the scientific theories they illustrate, this frank admission of emotional engagement comes as a surprise. Equally surprising, perhaps, is Jencks's insistence that his work is as close in spirit to ancient ritual sites, such as Stonehenge, as it is to cosmological theory.

In 2004 the Scottish National Gallery of Modern Art, in Edinburgh, won the Gulbenkian Prize for Museums for Jencks's design, Landform Ueda. Other recent and ongoing projects include the Black Hole landscape in the Beijing Olympic Forest Park, a DNA sculpture in Cambridge and the vast Northumberlandia, a landform in the shape of a woman, in northern England. The Spirals of Time project (now under construction), in the Portello district of Milan, is an urban park in the northwest part of the city that incorporates three major landforms: ponds, gardens and sculpture.

06

07

05–09 Spirals of Time at Parco Vittoria, in Portello, Milan (an area of the city traditionally used for car manufacturing), is a typically ambitious conceptual piece by Jencks that tells the story of human existence by means of interconnected circular garden zones, dedicated to pre-history, history, the present and the future. The project features a large lake with promontory, a DNA double-helix sculpture and spiral mounds.

08

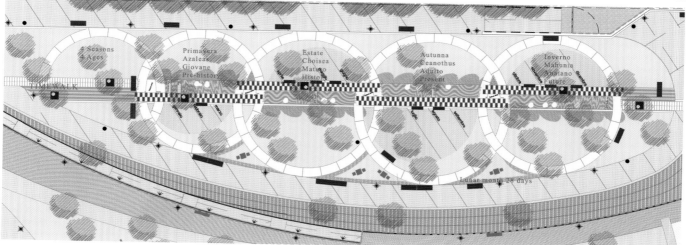

09

LANDSCAPE URBANISM
CHALLENGED

Perhaps we should start to think about urban landscape design in terms of gardening. The dreaded G-word, however, barely appears in the literature of landscape architecture.[1] It is viewed as irredeemably bourgeois 'decoration' that does not fit with the professional self-image of landscape architects, urban designers, town planners and architects. Gardens are for old people ('my parents'). Gardens are for right-wingers. Gardens are for social-climbing dilettantes or unsophisticated provincials. Gardens are embarrassing. Gardens are uncool.

Yet use Google Earth or any online satellite camera to zoom in on city neighbourhoods – particularly those in countries such as the UK and the Netherlands – and it is clear that private gardens make up a significant proportion of the green space in towns and cities. Gardens, both private and public, potentially have a big part to play in the urban landscape.

Indeed, perhaps urban landscape designers should start to think of themselves as gardeners of cities. After all, gardeners cannot get everything right; they cannot cover all the ground; they will have failures along with the unexpected successes; they are in partnership with a nature that can seem cruel and fickle, as well as benevolent and delightful; they would be unwise to make great claims for what they may achieve; they need to be content that nature will play a major role (perhaps the biggest role) in what they achieve as designers; they must discard the idea that a given site may be a zone for their own personal expression; and they must relinquish any fantasies of 'ownership' of what they design.[2] Gardening, therefore, provides a useful model and methodology. In this spirit, perhaps all landscape, including urban landscape, might be considered primarily in terms of people, place and plants.

People

The winning 'Tree City' entry in the 1999 competition for Downsview Park, Toronto, is often cited by landscape urbanists as a model proposition.[3] This was a joint submission by Rem Koolhaas and OMA, Bruce Mau, Petra Blaisse (of Inside/Outside) and Oleson Worland Architects. A key aspect of the brief was the concept of 'change over time', which was interpreted by the winning team as a slow evolution in three stages: site and soil preparation; pathway construction; and 'cluster landscaping'. The last is defined as 'a matrix of circular tree clusters covering 25 per cent of the site, which is supplemented by meadows, playing fields and gardens'. One of the chief perceived merits of the scheme was its relative cheapness – no expensive buildings or structures, with the rest of the park developing only as funding came on stream. None of the finalists in the competition made much reference to the fact that the park was being created on the site of a large former military airbase; in fact, it was not mentioned at all in the winning submission. Human history was therefore circumvented by a utopian ideal of a redemptive ecology, which exists only at the level of metaphor.

What about local residents, ex-employees and their relatives, the people who will use the park most? Are their memories of the military base simply going to be trashed and decorously overlaid by a pastoral simulacrum? People can emerge as oddly passive or absent when it comes to the radical transformation of places such as Downsview. Urban infrastructure is much discussed by landscape urbanists,[4] while the psychological and emotional infrastructure is often taken for granted or dismissed as unquantifiable. But such postindustrial sites retain their significance as workplaces despite their change in status. Indeed, it could be argued that such places become ever more important to local people as they gain a new identity and become a part of a community of memory. Most landscape companies who engage with postindustrial sites don't get much farther than thinking of them as redeemed, symbolically, by the presence of unbridled plantlife. This notion has some value as an underlying meaning to a project, but lacks sophistication and specificity. The German designer Peter Latz (see p. 138) is an honourable exception in that he has a much more sophisticated attitude (at projects such as the acclaimed Duisburg Nord), taking into account the emotional importance of such sites for local people.[5]

One of the most perceptive commentators on – and therefore formulators of – landscape urbanism is James Corner, a British designer who is also professor of landscape at the University of Pennsylvania and principal of Field Operations. Corner sees landscape urbanism as a new 'hybrid practice'[6] that spans architecture, landscape architecture, urban design and planning. Citing the social theorist David Harvey, Corner criticizes the 'formalism of the Modernist utopia and the sentimental, communitarian "new urbanism",' envisaging instead a utopia of process, rather than of form – 'how things work, interact and interrelate in space and time'.[7] Moving away from object-based realizations of design, Corner used the term 'recovering landscape' as the title for a collection of essays, referring not just to the rehabilitative aspects of urban landscape design, but the way it works through time, with change and mutability seen as something to celebrate rather than work against. Corner goes further than other landscape urbanists in positing a deeper, phenomenological role for designers, in the tradition of Martin Heidegger: 'It is becoming clearer that "space" is more complex and dynamic than previous formal models allowed. Ideas about spatiality are moving away from physical objects and forms towards the variety of territorial political and psychological social processes that flow through space. The interrelationships among things in space, as well as the effects that are produced through such dynamic interactions, are becoming of greater significance for intervening in urban landscapes than the solely compositional arrangement of objects and surfaces.' There is at least a possibility that human experience will, for landscape urbanists, be privileged among those 'interrelationships among things in space'.[8]

Place

When it comes to the concept of place, and more particularly, making places, some urbanists have announced the death of both functional Modernism and the death of meaning in design (discredited as part of the dastardly English 'pastoral/picturesque' model).[9] Yet it could be argued that conceptualist work, which contains commentaries, stories, narratives, symbols and so on still has an important part to play. At the same time, it should not be forgotten that landscape designers have a 'traditional' role as the creators of discrete, distinctive spaces within towns and cities. Such parks, plazas, squares, streetscapes and gardens can have an impact on the city and its residents far beyond their relative size. If, for example, we look at the tiny Paley Park in New York's Midtown (a 'pocket park'), it is plain that its impact on the psychic wellbeing of the city is far out of proportion to its size, ecological impact or integration with its surroundings.

With the dominance of the sustainability agenda, there is a kind of 'aesthetic cringe' occurring that has made the landscape/urbanist profession almost embarrassed about the concept of design for its own sake as a facilitator of human contentedness. Of course, just about everything architects, landscape architects, urbanists and city planners do is going to be ecologically unjustifiable and unsustainable by some measure, and compared with the realities of carbon emissions and other drivers of climate change, the impact on the global situation to be made by committed landscape urbanists – even those working on a town or city scale in places – will be negligible. They are essentially metaphorical gestures.[10] Which is not the same thing as saying a sustainable approach is a waste of time – it is simply that the rhetorical role of the sustainability agenda must be put in perspective. The issue of scale is also important. It appears that 'landscape urbanism' both privileges the large scale and seeks to flatten out traditional hierarchies of space in urban environments. Landscape urbanism is about marshalling, controlling and, to an extent, patrolling towns and cities, the implication being that every square inch of a city or town has equal potential value. This could lead to urban monotonies – an ecologically correct 'blandscape architecture' – or else the finessing of every corner so that there is no grime or grunge left for committed urbanites to revel in.

There might be something to be said for a landscape credo based on the idea of fragmentation and compartmentalization, as opposed to one founded on the idea of unification. Just as writer and activist Jane Jacobs made the compelling counter-intuitive argument that what cities require is greater residential density, not less, so a counter argument about urbanism might run that what is required is less consistency and rigour and more unpredictability – more variety, surprise and delight. Remember: Alexander Pope enjoined us to consult the genius of the place, not management-consult it. We like our cities to be made up of multiple 'personalities' (in terms of areas or neighbourhoods), which somehow coalesce to make up the personality of the whole city. And we like those personalities to be unregulated by the civic authorities.[11]

One contemporary extremity of eco-correctness manifests itself as a kind of self-appointed police force, which roams the urban realm looking for examples of good and bad practice. Organizations such as the Biomimicry Guild promote the idea that designers would do well to learn from the different ways in which plantlife cope with local conditions, and use that knowledge in their own work.[12] This is not uncontroversial. Such groups also offer local authorities and corporations a system of Ecological Performance Standards, in which they will measure any new design against the native ecosystem it has replaced – its soil fertility, water purity, air temperature, genetic diversity, pest control, CO_2 levels, and so on. One can imagine corporate and civic clients signing up to this in droves, driven by a potent mixture of ecological guilt engendered by the politically fomented terror of imminent eco-Armageddon, plus the good, old-fashioned profit motive – trees and plants are so much cheaper than buildings, playgrounds and other amenities. Of course, the idea of a 'self-cleansing' city (mainly thanks to tree plantation) is not new: the English plantsman Thomas Fairchild was making the same point in the early 18th century, though with no suggestion of this kind of compunction and moral pressure. One wonders, however, where good design might appear in this equation.

Playing into this is the role of urban ecology. We should cherish, too, those areas of cities that remain 'undesigned', left-over, marginalized. After all, this is where the ecology is really free to express itself. These are the spaces where weed communities grow, zones of natural distinction that may be decried as ugly, but at least provide some respite from the sense that we are being regulated by the authorities. Such spaces may only be temporary, subsequently 'developed' (or 'sivilized', as Huck Finn might put it), but every city needs a certain amount of such space for it to be able to breathe easily. Are all of these areas to be sucked into some all-embracing philosophy?

The High Line project in Lower Manhattan is a case in point: Field Operations' mantra of 'keeping it wild, quiet and slow' was posited as a way of keeping the essential atmosphere of the derelict railway line intact. The High Line was intended to be a train trip that got turned into a guilt trip. Yet, mercifully, the all-singing, all-dancing performance space that is the High Line today bears little resemblance, physically and atmospherically, to the wild and decrepit spaces it replaced. It is now a more or less manicured park (and very successful for that), not the succession of bogus 'wild' spaces that was originally promised.

Plants

The Australian critic and designer Richard Weller (see 'The Future of Landscape Design: Forum 1'; p. 240) has suggested: 'Perhaps landscape architecture is yet to

really have its own Modernism, an ecological modernity, an ecology free of romanticism and aesthetics.' The designers of the Sheffield School (see p. 268) come closest to this ideal now, with a methodology based on growing from seed versions of certain global plant communities identified as suitable, mainly in urban areas. What they present is a kind of 'expressive ecology', in which designers are not wholly passive in aesthetic terms, since they choose the plant mix to begin with, and intervene if it seems to be going awry in some way (for instance, if one species appears to be taking over). This expressive ecology could potentially become a much bigger part of our experience of towns and cities, in areas where it is deemed suitable: 'wilder' spaces, which complement more formally designed public spaces intended to fulfil different needs.

Such spaces could be small parks or open spaces in residential areas, green 'moments' in the busiest parts of cities, or elements that are built into new architecture or inserted into existing buildings. The crucial factor is the creation of an impression that such spaces are self-directing, once the plant communities have established themselves (though in reality the designers might be keeping quite a close eye).[13] Residents of towns and cities might then have a more palpable and authentic sense that they are living in and with nature, despite the fact that they are still surrounded mainly by buildings and roads (which will surely always remain the defining structures of cities, despite the fantasies of landscape urbanism). Any such notion of authenticity in terms of our relationship with nature would have to accept the principle that hitherto all recreations of nature in cities have essentially been ironic. By introducing expressive ecology into the urban environment, designers could establish a more authentic sense of balance between the urban environment and the natural world, improving daily life for residents while not actually claiming to be 'saving the planet' in any meaningful way.

It may be that landscape urbanism will prove to be a passing academic fad that has provoked a good deal of infighting. As the professional disciplines sort themselves out, it will probably become plain that the best approach is going to be collaborative, and that what citizens of towns and cities want is a wide range of design styles and attitudes at play in the environment in which they live – random-seeming 'expressive ecology' here, ideas-based conceptual design there. Variety will always be the spice of life, and of landscape – and, indeed, of urban design.

1 The exception that proves the rule being Chris Macdonald's essay 'Machines of Loving Grace', in *Center 14: On Landscape Urbanism*, ed. Dean Almy (Austin: The Center for American Architecture and Design, University of Texas at Austin, 2007): 205. Here he writes: 'The garden is a suggestive artefact in the formulation of an agenda for Landscape Urbanism insofar as it is, alongside agricultural practices, the cultural construct in which a balance between human desires and natural processes is sustained. In its engagement with cycles of time, in its need for sustained maintenance and renewal, and in its ability to entertain a rich variety of purposes, the project of the garden anticipates many of the concerns of Landscape Urbanism.' He goes on to note that 'the garden remains conspicuously absent from Modernist discourse'.

2 James Corner has embraced the prospect of error more fervently than the prospect of success (perhaps because he is British): 'In asserting authority and closure, current techniques have also failed to embrace the contingency, improvisation, error and uncertainty that inevitably circulate in urbanism.' 'The Agency of Mapping', in Almy, 171.

3 *Downsview Park Toronto*, ed. Julia Czerniak (Munich: Prestel Verlag, 2001).

4 Andrés Duany has sounded a valuable warning note about 'infrastructure': 'Landscape Urbanism's vaunted engagement with "infrastructure" amounts to buffering arterials, improving the design of storm-water apparatus, and decorating parking lots with porous paving. But an urban paradigm cannot be based on the implantation of natural vignettes in the residual places between buildings.' 'A General Theory of Sustainable Urbanism', in *Ecological Urbanism*, ed. Mohsen Mostafavi and Ciro Najle (Baden, Switzerland: Lars Müller Publishers, 2010): 407.

5 Norman Foster's city of Masdar in Abu Dhabi, which Rem Koolhaas cites approvingly in *Ecological Urbanism*, is a zero-carbon, zero-waste, zero-car city. It's a kind of Hobbesian utilitarianism. In the spirit of Swift's great satire *A Tale of a Tub* (1704), one wonders whether the real dream is for it to be zero-people, as well.

6 *The Landscape Urbanism Reader*, ed. Charles Waldheim (New York: Princeton Architectural Press, 2006): 23.

7 'The Agency of Mapping', in Almy, 157.

8 Ibid., 157.

9 This rejection of 'modern' and 'pastoral' in the search for modern landscape diction is a reversioning of the idea of 'middle landscape' defined by Peter G. Rowe in *Making a Middle Landscape* (Cambridge, Massachusetts: MIT Press, 1991).

10 The most striking example of hubristic exaggeration over sustainability comes from the back-cover blurb of Steffen Lehmann's ugly, unreadable and self-serving *The Principles of Green Urbanism: Transforming the City for Sustainability* (London: Taylor & Francis, 2010): 'This book shows how we can transform and future-proof the postindustrial city through strategies of architectural and urban design.' Future-proof?!

11 The old dichotomy between the urban and the rural is mutating into a dichotomy between built and unbuilt – or planned and unplanned – zones within towns and cities. As large cities come to dominate human culture more and more, and landscape planning engenders hierarchies that are themselves engendered by the quality of the physical fabric, this sense of division within urban centres will only increase.

12 This information is taken from Janine Benyus, 'Recognizing What Works: A Conscious Emulation of Life's Genius', in *What We See: Advancing the Observations of Jane Jacobs*, ed. Stephen A. Goldsmith and Lynne Elizabeth (Oakland, California: A New Village Press, 2010).

13 Street trees help fulfil this function, especially when they are allowed to express themselves – that is, grow into strange shapes that might even disrupt pedestrian flow.

MIKYOUNG KIM

BROOKLINE, MASSACHUSETTS, USA

Now a major player on the international scene, this is a firm bursting with confidence and innovative brio.

The output of Mikyoung Kim's eponymous firm ranges from garden and plazas to large-scale public parks and masterplans. Over the past sixteen years, Kim has created spatial narratives that encourage public interaction with art and the landscape. As an artist and design director, as well as professor in landscape architecture at the Rhode Island School of Design, she has brought both her background in sculpture and music and vision as a landscape architect to a wide range of projects. These comprise choreographed spaces and interactions, generated through an artistic, community-responsive process, and meld environmental design, sculpture and sustainable initiatives to develop 'engaging and poetic landscapes'.

The Barcode Luminescence project (2008) for the Ocean County Public Library in Toms River, New Jersey, was intended as a public space and visual landmark, symbolizing the knowledge and functions of the institution. Laser-cut steel lanterns act as beacons, guiding visitors to the entrance. The central plaza that fronts the library is located along the main thoroughfare, and was part of a new building that connected to the existing library. The addition focuses on integrating new technologies to convey information to the wider public, and, says Kim, 'draws together past and present, recognizing the well-travelled paths of the mobile institution, while reflecting the informational patterns of the library in the digital age'. The scope of the project included the courtyard design, as well as the design and integration of public art. Emphasizing movement and pathways of information, the criss-crossing paths reinforce connective relationships between the institution and the community. Integrated with the paved plaza are custom-designed lantern sculptures that illuminate the paths at night.

01

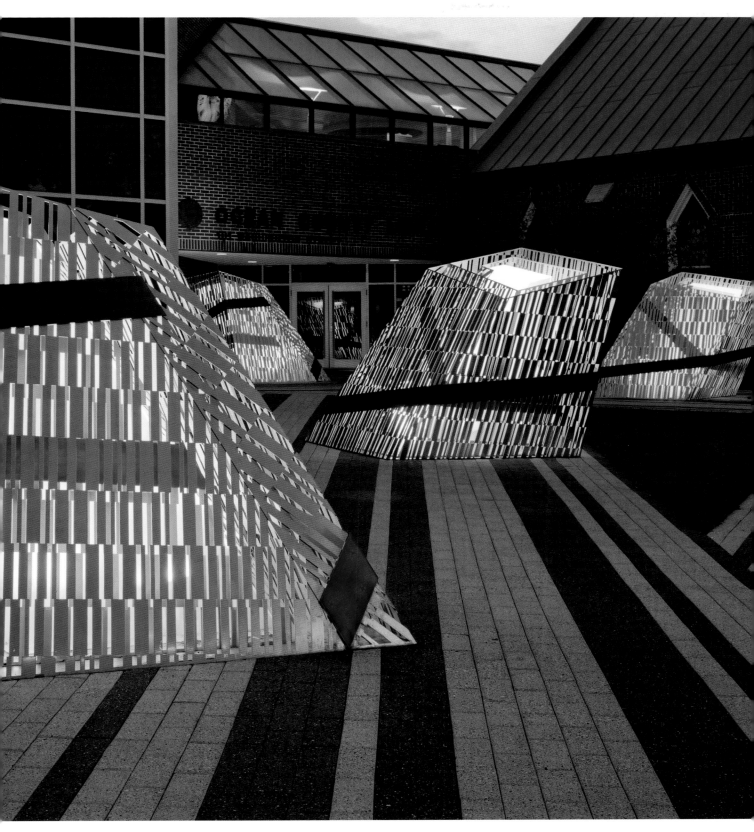

06

01 Barcode Luminescence at the Ocean County Public Library in New Jersey, where a series of lantern sculptures illuminate the entrance court at night. The 'barcode' patterns of the lanterns symbolize the transmission of data.
02 At the Farrar Pond project in Massachusetts, bluestone pavers set in linear patterns act as stepping stones, with moss and thyme planted between the 'open-weave' patterns.
03–05 The Flex-fence varies in height as it undulates in the landscape.
06 The line of the Flex-fence can be seen on the groundplan. The idea was to create a delimited area of 'garden' where the clients could enjoy a sense of safety and privacy, and where their dogs could run freely.

At a private residence at Farrar Pond (2008), in Lincoln, Massachusetts, near Henry David Thoreau's Walden Pond, the intention was to harmonize contemporary materials with the native plant palette and 'kettle and kame' (hills and depressions) geology, and to enhance the natural beauty of the site by using plants that would protect the existing ecological and watershed conditions. *Clethra alnifolia*, *Fothergilla major* and *Viburnum plicatum* create a shrub layer for screening and edge definition, while Siberian squill, snakeroot and lilacs offer multi-season colour at threshold zones. A grove of paper birch (*Betula utilis*) frames the main entrance to the driveway, while a secondary gateway of river birch (*Betula nigra*) is located in front of the main entrance to the house. Finally, a third birch grove weaves through a fence of Corten steel, and creates a visual dialogue with the existing trees that slope down to the pond. The sculptural Flex-fence, 30cm (12 in) thick and ranging from 1.2m (4 ft) to 1.8m (6 ft) in height, weaves in and out of the native hardwood forest and acts as a counterpoint to the solid retaining walls along the main drive. The fence system expands and contracts like an accordion; it was brought to site in its contracted position, and was then craned and unbolted so as to follow the changes in topography. Bluestone pavers were placed like stepping stones throughout the front entrance sequence and the driveway edging, so that all surfaces are pervious to run-off and drainage. The path moves under the fence and through the forest, allowing for the ground-plane materials to create rich transitions at key thresholds throughout the design.

In an urban context, Levinson Plaza (2008) in Boston, Massachusetts, provides a housing and development scheme with a landscape that draws its spirit from the regional gardens of New England. The plaza was intended to represent the convergence of community in the diverse, mixed-income complex. Design considerations included wind-, sound- and visual-screening (from the busy Huntington Avenue) by means of vegetation. Envisioned as an urban grove, the plaza provides an outdoor space for the residents, composed of all age groups and ethnicities. The pavement materials chosen will endure the long, challenging winters, while the patterning is based on the herringbone patterns of the local residential landscapes. The planting is composed of species that have been naturalized in the New England landscape, a palette of plants able to withstand demanding urban conditions: high winds, winter salt applications, poor soil conditions, and high variability of air and soil temperature.

07

08

07-10 The planting for Levinson Plaza in Boston
includes species such as birch and zelkova,
which have been naturalized in the urban
landscape of New England. The striking
ground-plane design echoes the traditional
herringbone paving in the surrounding
streets.

09

10

LANDSCAPE INDIA

AHMEDABAD, INDIA

An innovative and fearless firm, set to become a major player
on the international scene.

Landscape India was founded in the 1990s by Prabhakar B. Bhagwat, who also instituted the landscape architecture programmes at New Delhi University and CEPT University in India; most of the firm's thirty or so designers are also academics at these institutions. Bhagwat has been practising as a designer since 1973, and now his son, Aniket Bhagwat, is a leading light at the company. Little distinction is made between landscape and architectural projects, and, where possible, the firm takes on both elements of a project. Critiquing the homogeneity of contemporary culture, they state: 'We strongly believe that design values cannot be cloned or appropriated, but have to be created.' To this end, the firm has instituted an impressive range of research projects, also a reflection of the academic backgrounds of many of the practitioners.

For these designers, it is important that something of India's cultural distinctiveness is retained in the work of the firm. Aniket Bhagwat states: 'I think Indian architecture is doing just fine, but could show more life from time to time. The fact that we shy away from the kind of buildings and shapes that the world is building is a tribute to the fact that we are sensible and, in some sense, mired in and respectful of our cultural, economic and spatial context.'

Brick is one of the materials that characterizes Landscape India's design style; their own craftsmen fire bricks in special moulds, so that undulating, curved or coloured effects can be created. Traditional, compacted-earth floors and walls are used in a contemporary manner. The imaginative use of metalwork, poured-concrete flooring, stonework, wooden detailing and lighting design is also important, and can be achieved at a high level, thanks to the availability of skilled workmen in India.

01

01 The sunken mist garden at the Halfway
Retreat, outside Ahmedabad, is one of a
series of discrete garden episodes intended
to form 'a narrative of contrasts'.

Halfway Retreat (2008) is a weekend house on the outskirts of Ahmedabad where the landscape design has followed the architectural typology, which is based on the notion of discontinuity. What this means is that each part of the house has been designed as a discrete element. Landscape India designed the landscape with reference to three distinct ideas: the undulating topography; the linear nature of nearby agricultural fields; and a grid of trees that almost covers the property. A variety of courtyards have been introduced, all of them excitingly different to what has come before – there is a minimalist 'Eastern' garden of gravel and boulders alone, for example, as well as a wild garden of native grasses, terraced lawns and shady groves. The designers call this arrangement 'a narrative of contrasts'. Materials used in the architecture are vernacular in nature (mainly brick and stone), and in the garden every plant used is indigenous to the area, with most of them growing wild and therefore historically undervalued as garden subjects.

03

04

02-04 At the Blossom Industries industrial estate,
an extensive mango orchard forms a cool
and shady retreat.

Blossom Industries' new industrial estate (2009) in Daman was fashioned out of the site of an earlier business venture – a brewery – that had failed. It was a run-down set of buildings with no landscape. As Aniket Bhagwat explains: 'We decided to tell the story of many natures. Landscapes for industrial settings are usually bleak, workman-like compositions. The idea of art is rarely a dominant generative ideology. We decided to address that perception, too. We started with an installation at the entrance, a sculptural object with water that cascades down its textured sides, running in an elevated rill, then falling into containers out of two glass spouts. In one of these, the water is still and calm; in the other, it is frothy and bubbly – an allusion to the brewery.' Other artistic interventions include a series of four hugely enlarged versions of the brewery's cast-iron spigots, lining the entrance drive, and a massive steel 'drum', which bounds one side of a large lawn. The journey continues through a cool mango orchard planted with paspalum grass, and circles of lilies planted between the grid of trees.

08

05-07 Blossom Industries, where Landscape India boldly redesigned a brewery site as a venue for artistic expression. A semicircular steel wall forms a 'drum', encasing a large, raised area of lawn, while four stylized 'spigots' have been positioned by the drive.

08 The Aakash Party Plot is an updated version of a traditional 'aman', or wedding-party venue. Landscape India introduced an ambitious lighting grid and sound system, together with good kitchens and a range of appropriately festive decorative elements.

The Aakash Party Plot (2000) in Ahmedabad is a privately owned public space used for festivals and large gatherings, especially weddings. It is common for towns and cities to set aside land for this purpose, which must cater for between one and four thousand guests, though such spaces usually amount to little more than a dusty expanse of ground with a temporary shed as a kitchen. Aakash covers 1 hectare (2.5 acres) and can accommodate up to ten thousand people. The designers aimed to integrate into the space everything from parking and guest houses to a sound system and huge, suspended lighting grid. The walls bounding this green space are planted either vertically or on top. The whole ensemble is described as a 'high-energy collage'.

'We used a series of iconographic images that would help the mind connect to the idea of celebrations,' says Bhagwat. 'There are windmills and concrete canopies at entrance areas, glass "prayer wheels" that spin, screens with "eyes" cut out that watch people as they enter. And all the colours used are associated with festivities in India.'

LATZ + PARTNER

KRANZBERG, GERMANY / LONDON, ENGLAND

Well-established company known for its postindustrial designs,
still pushing the boundaries and experimenting with new ideas.

The three principal partners in this family-run operation are Peter Latz, who founded the firm more than forty years ago, his wife Anneliese and their son, Tilman. Best known for its work in postindustrial settings, the office's most celebrated venture is the much-documented Duisburg Nord project, a derelict steelworks resurrected as a public park in which nature and industry are held in balance. This holistic acceptance contrasts with the attitude to such sites of much of the landscape profession; there is often an attempt to posit nature as enjoying a kind of 'revenge' over industrial progress. Latz eschews this simple interpretation in favour of an approach that allows for the necessity of industry, and accounts for the complex feelings of locals towards sites that were until recently the long-term workplaces of many thousands of people.

The redevelopment of Kirchberg, in Luxembourg, originally laid out in 1961 on former agricultural land, is one of the office's biggest projects to date. A 'fundamental urban, landscape and artistic renewal' of the town was initiated at the beginning of the 1990s, with Latz providing the masterplan. Throughout the rest of the decade, and into the 21st century, Latz created three new parks: Parc Central; the Roman Road Park and European Arboretum; and the Dune and Water Park. In addition, the firm realized the transformation of the old motorway into a wide, tree-lined boulevard. Run-off from rainfall was channelled to become an essential element in the new parks. At Parc Central, rainwater from roofs and sealed surfaces flows into paved channels; before being fed into the lake, it gets circulated and is oxygenized by a water curtain, while a gravel reservoir beneath a meadow at the lake edge serves as a retention area. This combination of technology and aesthetics can also be seen at the Dune and Water

02

Park, in a small valley at the eastern city boundary. Surplus masses of road construction works form dune-like sculptures that enclose the park along the motorway.

At the Ariel Sharon Park, near Tel Aviv, the firm plans to transform the huge Hiriya landfill site into the centrepiece of a 800-hectare (1,977-acre) urban wilderness park. Two major components of the brief include the utilization of the Ayalon Plain as a flood-retention basin and the development of the encircling Mikveh Israel area as an agricultural enterprise. Seven million cubic metres (247,202,637 cubic ft) of soil will be displaced to create a basin that can withstand flooding over a seventy-two-hour period; the soil will then be added to the landfill mound to create a series of terraced earthforms that will act both as flood defences and as aesthetic features. The plan is for a nature reserve to evolve in the centre of the basin, which will contain permanent streams and streambeds that will only fill during heavy rainfall or the flooding season. A 'human corridor' will run around the lowest level of terraces, along a new canal and lake, towards a planned open-air amphitheatre to the north. These continuous belts will comprise promenades and water features between the wild heart of the park and the more artificial-looking terraces. The gently sloping terraces are covered with

01 Parc Central in Kirchberg, situated between the National Culture and Sports Centre, at the bottom left of the photograph, and the European School at the top right. Latz devised and implemented a masterplan for the town over a period of two decades.
02 The view from the lookout hill in Parc Central, towards the Sports Centre. This style of wall has been used for centuries in the vineyards of the Mosel Valley.
03 Allées and topiary in Parc Central, with the line of the converted motorway visible beyond.
04-05 The juxtaposition of traditional vernacular and modern materials is a feature of the new Parc Central.
06 The use of complementary formal geometries in tree-planting is a signature Latz move.

03

04

05

06

access

Ayalon

viewpoint

north terrace

viewpoint

green terraces
and water garden

catwalk

car access

access alley

Shappirim

hollow

open tableland

untouched slope of Hiriya

footterrace

recycling park

inside Ierradd

patterns that originate from existing agriculture on the site; orchards and olive groves follow the edges of the newly excavated flood plain, under whose shady canopies many activities can be integrated. The expressive topography of the park allows for 'introverted', quiet areas and numerous 'extroverted' places that will be windy and often noisy, but will also offer spectacular views. The vegetation will create a series of 'windows' along the road to enable views of the park and the landfill mountain.

Along with the essential question of how to store the water, there is the problem of how to clean it. The quality of the water will be enhanced by cleansing biotopes, to be installed wherever water flows into the park. Reservoirs that fill in winter secure the water supply for the sand filters during the dry summer months. Another important guarantor for the water quality is a side canal, or bypass, where a weir regulates the water inflow and leads the first, usually polluted water mass through the bypass, past the *wadi* (the Arabic term for a dry riverbed or valley) and into the direction of the concrete canal at the western edge. Only the clean, second flood is led to the central retention basin, where the water will be used to create a decorative spectacle in winter.

08

TOM LEADER

BERKELEY, CALIFORNIA, USA

Solidly performing yet continually developing company,
specializing in glamorous domestic settings.

After sixteen years as a partner with Peter Walker & Partners and a fellowship at the American Academy in Rome, Tom Leader formed his studio practice in 2001 in his living room. Leader's 'mission statement' is more like a heart-to-heart chat, and is worth quoting for that: 'Like many young practices, we shot for a high profile with a low overhead. We always seek a fresh, often alternative approach, to experiment with process, methods and materials. At the same time, we know what we're doing, who we're doing it with, and who else needs to be involved. Modes and fetishes are a distraction. Manifestos are boring. We are not landscape urbanists any more than we are digital prophets or protean art-makers, not that there's anything wrong with that! We like to know a client, what they seek and why they seek it. We like to know the community we are working in, because, even for a brief period, we always join them.'

Leader was a finalist in the competition to design the 1,821-hectare (4,500-acre) Shelby Farms Park (2008) on a former penal farm adjacent to a tributary of the Mississippi River, near Memphis, Tennessee. Bisected by a four-lane highway, the site was also broken in two by its use: a progressive land conservancy on the forested uplands, and an agricultural research farm servicing industrial food companies on the alluvial lowlands. Leader proposed linking the two sides physically with a series of land bridges, and programmatically with a large, organic produce farm that honoured the site's agricultural past. Both of these elements would span the highway. A 16-hectare (40-acre) reservoir was to be created, both to gravity-feed the farm and to allow recreation on its shores, including a new beach, esplanade and lakeside amphitheatre and centre for local music.

01

02

01-02 The competition entry for Shelby
Farms Park, near Memphis, envisaged an
agricultural theme in keeping with the site's
former existence as a penal farm. Leader's
idea was to revitalize the local economy
with the addition of an organic farm and
reservoir, along with semi-covered garden
spaces and a stage for rock concerts.

04   05   06

07

08

03-06 The new masterplan for Stanford Medical
School in California includes the landscape
around a Learning and Knowledge Center,
which features rectangular planting beds
and towering palms.
07-08 The Discovery Walk, conceived by Susan
Schwartzenberg, is lined with twenty-
three planters decorated with images that
illustrate the history of medical research
and teaching at Stanford.

Stanford Medical School in Palo Alto, California, commissioned Leader to formulate a masterplan for a new campus, including the landscaping around a Learning
and Knowledge Center (2010). After decades of being housed within the Edward
Durrell Stone-designed complex at Stanford Hospital, the Medical School is now
emerging with its own physical presence. Leader describes the studio's idea for the
masterplan: 'The overall plan created a tight, quad-like concentration of programme
and identity for the school, which is strongly joined to the original Stanford fabric by
a series of movement corridors across Campus Drive. These connectors organize the
entire campus internally with a "plaid" of linear spaces of varying scales.'

At the Learning and Knowledge Center, Leader created Alumni Green, a new
quadrangle that acts as a 'green living room' for the school, and a formal, palm-lined
entry way for vehicles and pedestrians. A medicinal herb garden provides extensive
seating and outdoor gathering spaces. Integrated into this scheme is a narrative art
project that is perhaps the signature feature of the design. The Discovery Walk stretches
north for nearly a kilometre (about half a mile) to create an organizational spine for
this part of the campus. Leader's proposition was to reveal a narrative history of medical research along its length, and he engaged local artist Susan Schwartzenberg to
develop the story. A series of tree planters, twenty-three seats high, are faced with four
hundred black granite panels, photo-etched with images and text as designed by the
artist. These create an expansive, detailed and often personalized and provocative
story about research and teaching at the university. Told through Schwartzenberg's
composition of historical images, interviews and factual research, printed on pre-cast
panels, the story unfolds along a ribbon of U-shaped benches and informal spaces.

LEVIN MONSIGNY

BERLIN, GERMANY

Effective, functional landscape and garden design enlivened
by surreal twists and unexpected moves.

This German–French partnership was founded in 1998 by Martina Levin, Nicolai Levin and Luc Monsigny, with Axel Hermening joining in 2001. They summarize their attitude as follows: 'We are united through our enjoyment of design and construction; the passion of discovering, taking in and deciphering new places; and the challenge of finding individual solutions for predetermined compositions. The result is therefore singular, and leads to an unmistakable identity of place.' Both Martina and Nicolai Levin worked as gardeners before training as landscape architects in Berlin, and, unusually among German landscape firms, claim that 'common to all of our designs is a dialogue concerning the most basic of the materials at our disposal: the plant'.

The company's highest-profile project to date is the design for Museum Island (2002), in Berlin, which complements the renovation and extension of the magnificent buildings as a 'sanctuary for art and science', a belated realization of the vision of Friedrich Wilhelm IV. The space is divided into three categories: streets as functional elements; open spaces as 'areas of reverie'; and railway lines as incisions in the urban fabric. Key sites are the cathedral garden next to the Altes Museum, the Kupfergraben plaza and new glass foyer, a sculpture garden near the Alte Nationalgalerie, and a plaza behind the Pergamon Museum. The areas directly beneath the railway lines will be covered with steel plating, and glass showcases will be installed between supporting columns to house exhibitions. The ever-changing geometry of the segments will be reflected by additional sheets of metal attached to the ceiling of the underpass. A ghostly light shining through incisions in the floor and ceiling will further accentuate the strangeness of the space. Viewing points set into the ground along a planned

01-02 The public spaces around the museums
and institutions on the restored Museum
Island, in Berlin, were designed as 'spaces
of reverie', united by the use of a local
sandstone.

04

03 The frontage of the Alten Kommandantur on Berlin's Unter den Linden, with Levin Monsigny's distinctive garden additions.

04 The semicircles were intended to complement the building's austere neoclassical façade, while creating a contrast in terms of materiality.

underground corridor between the museums, and transparent balconies at the ends of the narrow alleys at the Kupfergraben canal, provide further places of interest.

Elsewhere in the city – on the main thoroughfare, Unter den Linden – Levin Monsigny restored the frontage of the Alten Kommandantur (2004), which originally served as offices and living quarters for Berlin's military commandant and is now used as an office by media giant Bertelsmann. Its front gardens, which are built directly into the public pavement, were originally designed as a departure from the typology of the city's grand boulevards. This unique characteristic was reason enough for the firm to recreate the open-space theme of the gardens together with the building. The motif of two semicircular structures is a reference to historical plans by Karl Friedrich Schinkel, who had a decisive influence on the character of this urban space. The semicircles, which at first glance might seem out of place, are intended as an appropriate solution to the problems posed: their soft form tapers the broad pavement of the boulevard as it nears the Palace Bridge, directing pedestrian flow and simultaneously providing a generously framed and inviting entrance to the building. The clear, geometric shapes are designed to complement the severity of the Prussian architectural aesthetic. The gardens' surfaces are covered with shiny gravel, matching the building's façade. Low, metallic-edged verges assume the material of front-garden fencing, and are planted with rhythmically placed box hedges of differing hues.

LOHAUS CARL

HANOVER, GERMANY

Formally imaginative practice that dares to use an innovative vocabulary, setting them apart from many other Modernist design firms in Germany.

Irene Lohaus and Peter Carl established their office in 1996, and have enjoyed considerable success in both the public and corporate spheres. 'The history of a place is an important source when planning inner cities, squares, pedestrian precincts and street spaces, promenades, parks, landscape views, universities and hospitals, as well as residential areas, corporate premises and gardens,' say the partners. 'The stories that go with a place form the basis for our development of a concept.' The emphasis in their work is on the creation of simple yet coherent spaces that exude a sense of tranquillity, even if the environment itself is used in multiple or complex ways. They maintain that in such an atmosphere, it is possible to 'focus on subtleties in the landscape, to contemplate the essentials, or simply enjoy'. The argument is that a strong and well-thought-out landscape structure will resist minor changes and the ravages of time.

The Hartecenter (2005), in Hanover, is the property of Hanomag Lohnhärterei, a company that deals with the heat treatment of metals. The focus of the complex is a three-storey administration building that houses a cafeteria, located in front of the production hall. Lohaus Carl's design for the outdoor area has a playful atmosphere, in contrast to the functional character of the rest of the site, which is primarily used by lorries and heavy equipment. A chequered pattern consisting of areas of concrete plates, squares of lawn and steel plates gives the main entrance of the building an individual expression with a human scale.

On a much larger scale, the 55-hectare (136-acre) Westpark (ongoing) is the focal point of a new neighbourhood in the grounds of the former Reese and Sheridan Kaserne (a US Army officers' club) in Augsburg. The park forms a green corridor in

02

the western part of the city. Linking the various features of the park is a meandering footpath in light-coloured asphalt that also serves as a cycle-path, running north–south. Its width varies intermittently, and it occasionally separates to create new paths that drift apart and merge together again. Depending on the form of the paths, there are 'fast' or 'slow' connections from point to point. Between the ribbons of pathways are spaces that offer a variety of sport facilities and play opportunities, including hockey, in-line skating, BMX bike tracks and volleyball, as well as playgrounds for children. There are also displays of plant arrangements, from movable prairie perennial beds to artificial landscapes, which take the form of groups of hillocks. The existing trees are being conserved and enhanced with maples and other typically North American tree species that exhibit dramatic autumn colour. It was important to the designers that both the line of the central path and the amenities in the park be clearly delineated in terms of function; as such, there is no signage at all.

03

04

01 A small plaza in front of the administrative
building of a metal-treatment company in
Hanover: a nicely understated chequerboard.
02-03 Multiple pathways form ribbons that merge
and divide in Augsburg's new Westpark,
while a series of playful landscape spaces,
including a hummocked area, add constant
variety.
04-05 Children's playgrounds and quiet seating
areas provide a wide variety of experiences
in the park, which succeed each other in a
carefully planned sequence.

05

MCGREGOR COXALL

SYDNEY, AUSTRALIA

Leading landscape architecture firm with a string of exciting
recent projects, specializing in industrial regeneration.

Adrian McGregor and Philip Coxall trained together at the Environmental Design
School in Canberra in the 1980s, and pursued separate careers before joining forces in
2000. The partners describe themselves as 'proponents of a new wave of environmentally focused landscape architecture, framed within a Modernist design approach
[that] blurs the boundaries between culture, design and ecology'. The office pursues a
rigorous process of contextual investigation, and as a result, the partners say, will often
challenge the client brief during the design process. In addition, their projects propose
the use of sustainable technologies and systems to reduce energy consumption,
manage water recycling on site, reduce maintenance costs and minimize any effects
that might damage the natural environment.

The duo's most celebrated commission to date is Ballast Point Park (2009), a 2.5-
hectare (6.2-acre) postindustrial waterfront park created on the contaminated site of
a former lubricant production plant on the Birchgrove Peninsula, in the inner reaches
of Sydney Harbour. The site's richly layered history included occupation by indigenous people, construction of the Menevia marine villa in the 1860s, quarry use for
ship ballast, and finally petroleum distillation from the 1920s until 2002. The design
philosophy was to acknowledge the site's past history, while providing a park for the
future. The new park features on-site energy production, generated by eight vertical-
axis wind turbines on a contemporary structure that replaces one of the old site's
larger fuel storage tanks. Concrete, brick and crushed building material provide the
fill for sculpted gabion walls, which retain a sequence of stepped viewing terraces with
sweeping views. Thirty-four thousand plants grown from locally collected seeds will

02

03

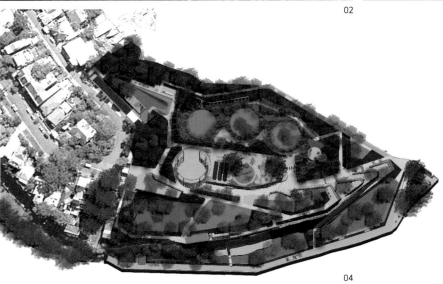

04

05

06

01 Gigantic gabions containing recycled
   materials contrast with the natural rock
   at Ballast Point Park in Sydney.
02-06 The aesthetic of this striking park is created
   by the reuse of the industrial facilities,
   including vast storage tanks that have
   been redeployed as viewing platforms
   and walkways. There are fine views back
   to Sydney Harbour and its bridge.

eventually clothe this headland in green, and elegant reinterpretations of the old Caltex petroleum site staircases provide dramatic linkages between the site levels. Ponds containing wetland plants clean the site-water prior to its entering the harbour, and also provide a habitat for birds and frogs. The designers state that their plan 'aims to minimize the project's carbon footprint and ecologically rehabilitate the site, reconciling historical layers within a framework of contemporary sustainability, in which recycled materials are used in innovative ways to create a low-carbon park. Thus the new park combines interpretations of the site's cultural heritage with environmental innovation to recreate a green headland for use by the local community.'

Among the sustainable elements in the design is the planting (using local flora), storm-water biofiltration, and the use of recycled materials and wind turbines for renewable energy. Compacted waste material from the site was reused to form reinforced earth walls, with recycled rubble deployed as a facing material to these walls, recycled aggregates for drainage and edging, recycled soils and mulch, recycled timber for seats, decking and building walls, and the use of eco-concrete, which utilizes recycled aggregate and slag as a substitute for cement in the concrete composition.

At the National Gallery of Australia in Canberra, built in 1983, McGregor Coxall were involved in a major refurbishment (2010) that included a new building entry, expansion of the galleries, a function room and the creation of southern gardens. The gallery expansion and public domain works link to the adjacent Australian High Court and the National Portrait Gallery, completing an ensemble of arts and civic facilities in the Parliamentary Triangle.

The New Australian Garden and the building extensions were intended to portray the story of Australian art from its origins, placing the continent's earliest cultures as its entrance. On plan, the firm extended the triangular grid of the original building to create a framework for the location and arrangement of significant design elements, such as pathways, bridges, walls and water elements. Located on the site of the former car park, the main garden is designed around existing mature eucalyptus trees. Two planar lawns form the main space, creating an 'inside–outside' room of huge proportions. These lawns were designed to host functions and events, including temporary art exhibitions and garden parties. Native slate and granite, concrete aggregates and gravel sourced from local quarries are consistent with the material palette of the existing works. Extensive indigenous planting was used to support the eucalyptus trees to form a dense frame of bushland around the geometrically designed lawns. Storm water is harvested from all external areas and roofs for internal reuse and irrigation of the new garden. 'Our intention was to make a timeless contribution to the site,' say the team, 'to add space, light and texture, but without clutter.'

07-11 The New Australian Garden, on the site of a former car park, is now focused around a large pool that contains a subterranean skyspace by James Turrell. Existing eucalyptus trees were retained, while the pristine panels of lawn can be used for parties and other functions.

09

10

11

MESA DESIGN GROUP

DALLAS, TEXAS, USA

A large international company that has not lost its creative edge,
allowing individual designers their voices.

This large company, based in Dallas with satellite offices in three more countries,
retains a distinctive style, seen in designs that range from small garden spaces to large-
scale masterplanning projects. Their philosophy has been honed since the company
was founded in 1981, and is one of the most succinct and coherent out there: 'On every
project, Mesa strives to build livable, sustainable environments that balance human
needs and natural beauty, while understanding and respecting the ecosystem supporting each site. Our projects reflect these goals by revealing the presence and character
of the natural environment, producing an organically inspired overlay of local cultural influences, evoking a human response by creating a unique sense of place, inter-
weaving positive human interaction and natural beauty into the fabric of a community,
transforming materials into appropriate and compatible forms, proportion and scale,
offering each visitor the chance to experience something larger and more spiritual
than the individual, and investing our passion by creating an emotional response in
the people who use this place.'

The studio was asked to revamp the gardens at the Oak Court Residence (2008),
in Dallas, an International Style building designed by Edward Durrell Stone in 1957
using brise-soleil. The garden had originally been designed by Thomas Church, who
had also integrated two pools inside the house itself. The exterior strictly followed the
building grid and did not incorporate pathways. The main entrance and motor court
were rearranged by Mesa so that the central focal point again conforms to Stone's
exterior grid, which is the basis for the entire design. The central lawn plinth, 12.2m
(40 ft) in diameter, features a large sculpture by the Colombian artist Fernando Botero.

01

02

03

01 The serene men's courtyard by moonlight, at the Oak Court Residence in Dallas. Plants include fig ivy, dwarf mondo grass and black bamboo. The hard surfaces are crushed-marble gravel and a circle of black granite.

02 The women's courtyard is a quiet space, containing Japanese maples and a ring of white limestone, filled with 'fibreoptic grass' (*Isolepis cernua*).

03 A sculpture by Fernando Botero now forms the centrepiece of the motor court. One of its functions is to obscure views of the street from the house interior.

04

04 The geometric groundplan extends across
   both house and garden.
05 The far end of the women's courtyard.

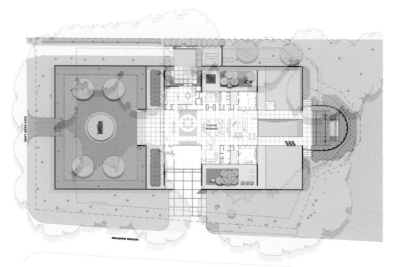

05

Two allées of pleached Japanese maples in 'rugs' of dwarf *Ophiopogon japonicus* animate the space with seasonal colour and sculptural branch structure. The rear garden was originally considerably larger, with views down to a creek. Mesa shrouded the new back wall with bamboo and introduced an elevated limestone terrace, flanked by water. Although the creek views are gone, the client now enjoys a private outdoor living room, swimming pool and spa. The exterior grid-pattern extends across the entire lot, including the men's and women's sculpture courtyards on either side of the house. The idea of these separate spaces stems from the former men's and women's first-floor dressing rooms near the indoor swimming pool. It was also, perhaps, a reference to the 'gendering' of the different sides of houses in European architectural tradition (at the late 17th-century Dutch royal palace of Het Loo, for example).

The courtyards, a yin-yang reflection of each other, use contrasting materials. The men's courtyard shares a glass partition wall with the first-floor library, men's restroom and guest room. The space is serene, reflective and spare. Plants include a lone Japanese maple, salvaged during construction, a stand of black bamboo within a circle of artistically placed chunks of black granite, a carpet of dwarf mondo grass, and fig ivy on a white stucco wall. Crushed-marble gravel and black granite form the ground plane, which features a fountain, also made from black granite. The women's courtyard borders the first-floor music room, ladies' powder room and second guest room. The space contains female-form sculptures, Japanese maples, 'fibreoptic grass' (*Isolepis cernua*), dwarf mondo grass and more crushed-marble gravel. An open seating arrangement of furniture designed by Richard Schultz sits opposite the glass wall of the guest room, edged on one side by seasonal plants in custom-designed stainless-steel planters. Although adhering to the grid, the women's courtyard is softer and brighter, a contrast to the hard-edged lines of its 'male' counterpart.

06-07 Beck Park, in Dallas, was conceived as a series of outdoor rooms delineated by water, concrete walls, Pennsylvania bluestone pebbles and maple trees. The water level in the reflecting pools is flush with the plaza.

08 Changes of level help create moods of intimacy and privacy in this 'pocket park'.

09-11 At the House by the Creek, near Turtle Creek, a 'fountain' wraps round the dining terrace, with water spilling out of the top level and down the wall into a channel below.
12 The garden is an interpretation of the naturally occurring limestone outcroppings along the creek, which the landscape architects matched in a new path.
13 A lawn panel seems to flow off the terrace, down the planted steps and onto the level below to form a soft, even lawn space. Such spaces were intended by Mesa to form areas of connection between the house and garden and the natural surroundings.

Beck Park (2004) is located in the heart of downtown Dallas, near the city's museum and the Nasher Sculpture Center. A 'pocket park' in the spirit of New York's celebrated Paley Park, it was built to celebrate the life of Henry C. Beck, Jr., founder of Beck Construction. The adjacent building houses the Fashion Industry Gallery and a restaurant, as well as the company's headquarters. The design was conceived as a series of Modernist outdoor 'rooms'. A shady grove of trees with tables and chairs for lunch breaks is the largest of these rooms, with the smallest one a quiet and contemplative space. Few materials were used, only water, concrete with both a smooth and bush-hammered finish, Pennsylvania bluestone (both as slabs and crushed), aggregate, bronze for the railings and simple, integrated wood seats. The plant choices and their placement are also intentionally spare and specific, with turf at the sloped lawns under the existing large live oaks, English ivy at the base of walls, and a mass of October Glory maples concentrated at the interior court.

The House by the Creek (2006) sits on a wooded lot in Highland Park, an established Dallas neighbourhood bordered by Turtle Creek. Mesa designed a quiet woodland garden in which 'the outdoor spaces', they say, 'disengage from their rectilinear forms into the geometries of nature as they move from the building's edges and patios, reaching towards the creek'. Yet this property next to a busy four-lane road feels serene because of the heavy tree cover and the siting of the house itself. This project uses high-quality materials in a low-key way, so that they blend easily with the landscape: slate from India, Texas limestone, almondrilla wood, stainless steel and copper.

12

13

TERESA MOLLER

VITACURA, CHILE

Environmentally sensitive design that integrates elements of the natural landscape, while incorporating complementary materials.

The incomparably varied landscapes of Chile have been the setting for the projects of Teresa Moller's studio. A variety of distinct palettes of plants and materials are utilized, since project locations range from the Atacama desert in the north to the Lakes Region in the south, the Pacific Coast in the east to the Andes mountains in the west. Moller approaches each garden by studying the surrounding landscape, architecture, animals and natural systems. As a result of this research, her designs incorporate clean lines, linear movements and a wide range of native plantings. Moller seeks to 'provide a point of interaction between humans and nature' within her gardens, working across the realms of residential, urban, commercial and agricultural settings.

Punta Pite (2006) is an 11-hectare (27.2-acre) site in central Chile, 145km (90 miles) north of Santiago, where an arm of the Cordillera de la Costa is submerged in the sea in the form of rocks, beaches and a scrub-forested valley. Each coastal settlement in Chile requires a public footpath along the coast, and this project involved designing twenty-nine different sections of path. Moller's intention was to reveal the natural landscape, rather than intervene in it, so she was careful to ensure that she provided a path only where nature's own route proved unsuitable for human traffic. The construction of the project demanded care and sensitivity, and some forty skilled stonemasons were employed to work on site. The same ethos was adopted for the creek, which is forested with the native flora. Moller wanted to bring people in to this strip of virgin forest, and began creating a system of walkways that lead up the creek. She collaborated with the sculptor Aristide, who created the Gerardo stones that were placed under existing *Cupressus macrocarpa* trees or amid a colony of native orchids.

01-03 At the Punta Pite project, in central Chile, Moller created a series of steps and pathways to create a route along a rocky coastline. The rationale was to intervene as little as possible in the natural landscape.

04–06 At this private residence in the Pirque region of Chile, Moller made reference to the agricultural traditions of the area through the use of local materials and the adoption of an orchard motif as the central theme.

04

05

In Pirque (2005), a predominantly agricultural region of Chile, a young couple wanted a weekend house away from the hustle and bustle of Santiago. The idea of working the land was key to the brief, while the budget demanded a simple design. Moller began with the design of the orchard, a linear approach in which contrasting textures were created by juxtaposing strips of mown and longer grass. The result is a strongly textured landscape, which accentuates the beauty of the various fruit and nut trees found on the property. Moller sought to use an agricultural vocabulary when creating other spaces in the garden. The fence along the property's northern boundary was made from walnut prunings that had been discarded by neighbouring farmers (much to their amazement); the wood has now silvered and is seen as a way of relating the site to the traditions of the region. Moller enjoys using whatever comes to hand; in some cases, clients were expecting the removal of 'waste' products that were instead used to create a dominant feature in the garden. Here, Moller reused rocks unearthed during construction of the house, which she then placed beneath the bowed branches of fig trees, creating hidden areas to discover.

06

N-TREE

TOKYO, JAPAN

A truly individualistic take on the tradition of Japanese design, courtesy of an original sculptural sensibility.

Takeshi Nagasaki, the founder of N-Tree, calls himself an 'art gardener'. Having studied at Tokyo University of the Arts and spending two years in Spain to study painting, Nagasaki returned to Japan to work with woodcuts and sculpture, while at the same time embarking on a degree in landscape studies. In 1997 he formed N-Tree, and ten years later relocated to London, moving back to Japan in 2011.

When creating art for the garden, Nagasaki sets out to 'transpose the essence of deep meditative thought into the beauty of natural form'. His intention is not to create nature by sculpting it, but to preserve nature by 'casting' it. For Nagasaki, using materials such as bamboo, leaf and stone, and changing their material state into glass and bronze, represents a kind of rebirth, giving light and energy back to the garden. These art objects also represent a kind of 'memento' for the garden, which, he says, contains within it a profound appreciation of beauty.

The Black Soil and Hexagon Garden (2008) is located in Oiso, Japan, a resort town surrounded by hills, with beaches and a shallow sea to the south. The garden was designed for the Morita family, who have run a chemist's shop from the premises for generations, and who felt the town had lost much of its greenery. Nagasaki describes his design as a modern stroll garden (*kaiyuu-shiki-teien*), and as a means of reaching back into the past to create something that once existed for his clients. The shape of the garden is extremely unusual, with acutely angled corners turning in on themselves to create triangular spaces, which Nagasaki treated as separate episodes in the narrative. The principal focus is a garden house, with walls of burnt cedar and a horizontal deck, though the black volcanic soil used as the basis of the garden perhaps creates the

02

overall tone. Nagasaki has followed traditional stroll-garden methodology by creating multiple viewpoints in a relatively small area, increasing the sense of space within it. Walling is the principal means by which the views have been created, while elements such as the pillars of the garden house also serve as framing devices. Nagasaki worked closely with the architect Motoji Wada on the design of the garden. In the centre, an area of black soil was designed as an open sun-trap, to contrast with the more enclosed parts of the garden. A six-sided slab of decorative concrete is a reference to the surrounding mountain range, while a serene water feature is intended as a homage to the character of the sea. A large, irregularly shaped window in the garden house was created partly as a means of viewing the lighting design by Fumio Mizukawa. Among the trees planted are *Fraxinus lanuginosa f. serrata*, *Ilex pedunculosa* (a Japanese holly), *Acer palmatum* 'Matsumurae', *Cornus kousa* and *Prunus mume f. pendula*. Colour comes from rhododendrons, pieris, spiraea and other shrubs, while the groundcover is provided by aspidistra species, three kinds of ophiopogon grass and mosses.

01-02   At the Black Soil and Hexagon Garden in Oiso, an irregular six-sided slab and fragmented stone path through black soil acts as a reference to the surrounding landscape.
03-05   Nagasaki's artwork *Decked in Green* at the L Residence, in Regent's Park, London, in a raised garden designed to be viewed from a terrace in the traditional Japanese manner.

03

04

05

OAB

BARCELONA, SPAIN

Exuberant landscape design, unbounded and unbracketed,
from the office of Carlos Ferrater.

Carlos Ferrater established the Office of Architecture (OAB) in 2006 with Xavier Martí, Lucía Ferrater and Borja Ferrater as creative partners. Best known as an architect (the Auditorio de Castellón; the Aquileia Tower in Venice; and the Olympic Village, Catalonia Convention Centre, Scientific Institute and Botanical Garden, all in Barcelona), Ferrater and his colleagues have been increasingly working in the sphere of landscape design. Current projects include a landscaping intervention in the Atapuerca archaeological site in Burgos. As they put it: 'OAB combines the experience of a recognized innovator architect and the strength of a young company, nowadays expanding with great success. The youth and eagerness of our team have enabled us to complete projects of great complexity, both in form and structure.'

OAB's redesign of the seafront at Benidorm (2009), in Spain, is the company's most dramatic landscape design to date. Benidorm is emblematic of Spanish tourism, a city of extremely high density concentrated in a tiny area. This dense model has, in fact, shown itself to be more efficient and sustainable than larger developments that require the destruction of huge tracts of land, creating towns that are empty for nine months of the year and are almost impossible to maintain. In the competition for the remodelling of the 1.5km- (0.9 mile-) long West Beach Promenade, OAB proposed a new design 'with a life of its own'. This concept is symbolized by organic lines all along the seafront, which also act as a reminder of the natural wave forms that generate an ensemble of honeycombed surfaces along the coastline, creating light and shadow, platforms and levels. In this case, an evocation of those natural processes create areas for play, meeting, leisure or contemplation. The construction of the promenade allows

01

01 The design for a new promenade at
    Benidorm took the formation of the natural
    coastline as its inspiration, with jutting
    promontories and different levels organized
    along organic lines.

02-07 Coloured tiles create a jaunty atmosphere
    at this holiday destination, and the
    numerous stairways take visitors down
    to beach level. The lower level also acts
    as a transition area between the beach
    and the town's underground car parks.

08 At this twin company headquarters in Barcelona, the exterior spaces segue seamlessly with the architecture to create a minimalist platform that acts as a buffer between the two buildings. With the railway line so near, this is less of a 'garden' and more of a meditative space for employees to gaze onto from their offices above.

for the natural run-off of rain- and seawater, so that traditional barriers against the sea have not been necessary. The promenade also links the beach with the resort's underground car parks, and has thus become a complex strip of transition between town and beach. Its surfaces intersect, move off and change level, generating jutting platforms and convex and concave shapes without ever encroaching onto the beach itself. The metaphoric model for the design is that of fabric, as the designers explain: 'The curved fabrics are gradually plaited and woven together, obtaining forms of fusion by following a few rigorous geometric norms.' The bright colours of the tiles (which won an international award) create a kind of abstract geography and help aid orientation. Just one material – white concrete – was used to construct the promenade and realize the various shapes of the benches and street furniture, which could then be clad in a variety of coloured tiles and other materials.

By way of contrast, OAB's architecture and landscape design for the corporate headquarters of GISA and FGC (2009), in Barcelona, is extremely minimalist and sober in tone. In terms of material, the exteriors of the two main buildings in this complex are realized in tinted glass and extruded, anodized aluminium, while the principal exterior space, in the area between the two structures, is a simple platform of concrete slabs, with the addition of narrow rectangular planters and skylights in a uniform arrangement. The skylights are lit at night, giving the space an attractive visual aura in an area where spending time outside is not a popular proposition due to the presence of the main railway line, just metres away.

THE RESURGENCE
OF LANDFORM

One of the most interesting formal trends in landscape design over the past decade or so has been the resurgence of interest in landform: shaping the earth into grass berms, terraces and mounds; and creating complementary pools of water. The subtle pleasure of landform lies in the play of light and shadow on the grass – during the passage of the seasons, or even across the trajectory of a single day. At dawn, the indistinct blue-grey forms of a turf sculpture gradually take on life as the sun reaches it. Droplets of dew catch the rays and twinkle like thousands of tiny spotlights, and the whole scene begins to warm up and glow. Frost will have its effect, of course, but a high-summer dusk can be equally beguiling, as the sharp edges of the grassed forms meld with each other as day dissolves into night. And even in the uncompromisingly strong light of midday, the many and varied shadows can come alive and create intriguingly intense patterns on the green canvas.

Landform has been a factor in the landscape for millennia, but in the mid-1990s it was given a new fillip through the example of the architectural historian Charles Jencks (see p. 110). Inspired by the landscaping experiments of his late wife Maggie Keswick, Jencks devised an astonishing landform garden at their estate in Scotland. The intellectual basis was an amalgam of all the latest cosmological theories, in that the central move – a magnificent S-shaped grass berm, offset by pools – was intended to mimic the form of the fractal, or the fractional dimension that exists between the dimensions, representing pure energy. Whether or not one understood the scientific underpinnings of this garden (and most did not), the sheer tactile pleasure of walking these mounds made it one of the most notable gardens of the late 20th century. It took a while for Jencks's influence to percolate, for the style seemed so much his own. But in the new century a number of other designers, including Kim Wilkie (see p. 330) and Dan Pearson (see p. 214), have made landform a key element of their visual vocabulary. In some cases, this has just been a matter of empty fashion. But the best designers are by no means mere copyists, and have made an attitude towards landforming very much a part of their own sensibility.

The historical context

Throughout human history, land has been reformed for a variety of reasons: practical, aesthetic, symbolic, ritualistic, spiritual, artistic, military. The most ambitious ideas of all were those of the architect Bruno Taut, who in his book *Alpine Architektur* (1919) suggested the reworking of an entire mountain range (recutting the peaks and studding them with coloured glass), the redesign of certain Pacific Island groups, and the topographical restructuring of the earth and the decoration of the distant stars. Such bold ideas are beyond the purview of this essay, as are natural land formations and manmade landscape gardens that 'borrow' natural landscapes, including the borrowed-landscape traditions of China and Japan, and the 'borrowed views' employed in 18th-century English landscape-making.

Landforming by human beings dates back to prehistory. We cannot be sure of the significance of the shapes of the ancient burial barrows on Salisbury Plain, or of mounds in the Ohio prairie that were shaped like animals of cultural importance to the native tribes. Similarly, the precise meanings behind the Andean step terraces aligned on the stars or the lines of the Peruvian desert can only be guessed at. But we do guess, and in the process we falsify them. There is no doubt that these ancient earthforms somehow take on huge significance. Perhaps it is simply the passage of time. In the past forty years or so, land artists have engaged with such places, including Richard Long, who spent six days walking around the Cerne Abbas hill-figure in 1975. Even landform that originally served a purely practical end – like the ridge-and-furrow patterns created by medieval strip-farming in Britain, or the earth structures that organize villages in East Africa – can take on a spiritual dimension for the modern observer.

The Eastern tradition of landform

The first garden culture to incorporate large-scale earth-moving was that of China. In the earliest imperial gardens (around AD 100), the entire kingdom was encapsulated in parks as 'five lakes, four seas and five mountain peaks'. Later, specific landscapes were recreated in gardens and parks in what was called the 'mountain and water' style, incorporating undulating islands, decorated with rocks and sited on still lakes (one Chinese word for garden-making translates simply as 'digging ponds and piling hills'). Garden-makers were often also painters, and an aesthetic evolved in which gardens would 'unfurl' before the viewer like a scroll painting, in strict linear succession. Views were artfully framed, like pictures, in windows or gates, and artificial rock formations were realized in imitation of brush strokes.

Ancient Daoist texts described hills as the bones of the earth, water as the blood or arteries, and plants as the hair. The Chinese placement of numerous buildings among mounds in a garden is a reflection of the principles of man in harmony with all nature; artificial mounds also served a practical purpose, as sites for viewing pavilions. During the Sung dynasty (960–1279), one catalogue of rocks was printed that illustrated 116 different types, while an anonymous painter and garden designer categorized mountains thus: 'The spring mountain with misty clouds makes people active and happy; the summer mountain, covered with shady forest, makes people peaceful and poised; the autumn mountain, with bare tree trunks, makes people serious and solemn; and the winter mountain, with obscure views, makes people passive and lonely.' Environmental psychology avant le lettre.

Rockwork and landform was an aesthetic in itself. For Ji Cheng, the Ming dynasty garden-maker and author of the *Yuan ye* manual (1634), rocks and water were the most important aspect of the garden: 'Build up mountains from the excavated soil and form embankments along the edges of the ponds. High mounds can be further heightened and low-lying places should be dug deeper still.' He does not mention plants at all. Hills in Chinese gardens were usually asymmetrical, with a precipice on one side. This was the easiest method of construction, since one could walk up the shallower slope. Few soil-only mounds were made, and rocks often protruded decorously from the mounds. A whole rockwork style evolved based on the yin-yang contrast between gnarled, natural rock and smooth screen wall (the stone forest of Yunnan province was the most celebrated natural inspiration for this style).

The Chinese garden style was imported wholesale into Japan, but that ancient culture was also producing its own distinctive modes of earthworking, notably the Buddhist image of Mt Fuji as the centre of the universe (hence the 'mini Fujis' in Japanese gardens), and the creation of smooth mounds of white gravel that were designed to be viewed by the light of the moon. Japan's stroll-garden tradition called for considerable landforming to create perfect landscapes in miniature, or associations with famous landscapes, poems or paintings. The Japanese landform style can be described as more abstract than the Chinese tradition, and something of that spirit was summed up by the great designer Sōami, who wrote on the making of hill gardens, c. 1500: 'However small the garden may be, it can be made to include high mountains many miles away, and to create waterfalls of tremendous height.'

The Western tradition of landform

In the West, we find earthworks in medieval gardens in the form of turf seats, raised terraces and mounts – features that survived until the 18th century. Like the Chinese artificial hill, the mount served both a practical and decorative purpose, providing views outside the boundaries of the garden, and serving as a belvedere for viewing hunting in the park. Italian Renaissance gardens were often dramatically sited on hillsides, as per Alberti's advice, so it was a matter of creating terraces to cope with the slope, rather than moving earth. In 1505 Bramante demonstrated the desirability of changes of level in garden spaces with his Cortile del Belvedere at the Vatican, ostensibly the first architecturally designed outdoor space. Through the use of retaining walls, balustrading and steps, Bramante pioneered a convincing 3D aesthetic for garden design, and instigated a new set of perogatives for earth-moving in the context of the architecture of the corresponding buildings.

André Le Nôtre's geometric designs in the 17th century and their effect on the shape of the land reflected both the prevailing Cartesian philosophy of a universe underpinned by a fundamental orderliness, and Louis XIV's territorial ambitions and use of Versailles as a propagandic tool. The design of Le Nôtre's earth bastions, ditches, canals and terraces were directly lifted from the latest theories of military engineering (Vauban's defensive fortress system, especially). Some of his designs closely resembled the plans for fortified terraces in the French military manual, *The Art of War* (1684), the frontispiece of which shows gentlemen on a balustraded garden terrace with a battle happening in the background.

The early 18th-century landscape school in England gave rise to a whole new style of decorative earthwork. Charles Bridgeman's tiered amphitheatre at Claremont, in Surrey, provided landscape drama and a frisson of the Grand Tour, while at Sir Francis Dashwood's sexually charged West Wycombe Park, in Buckinghamshire, the phrase 'the earth moved' becomes appropriate in the context of the now-vanished Temple of Venus. Sir William Chambers's original design for Kew, on the other hand, packed full of architectural episodes in multifarious styles (from Chinese pagoda to Dutch house), suffered because the site is so boringly flat. Early 18th-century English landscapers used landform to enhance associative meanings, but later in the century 'Capability' Brown changed the shape of the ground for aesthetic reasons alone. Earth-moving was expensive and time-consuming, so Brown tended to reshape the land in conjunction with excavating a lake (just as the ancient Chinese did). At Blenheim Palace, for example, the spoil created through the enlargement of the lake round Vanbrugh's bridge was used to create more undulations.

The advent of the public park in the 19th century and the development of an avowedly 'picturesque' style called for earth-moving for a range of aesthetic and practical effects. At Derby Arboretum, one of the first public parks, J. C. Loudon's plan precisely specified the topography, while the success of Frederick Law Olmsted's Central Park in New York is dependent on its topography, natural and otherwise, and is notable for the use of artificially sunken roads to curb the impact of traffic. The last century has seen the self-conscious use of landform as a tribute to earlier landscape traditions, as in Beck & Collins's Innisfree Garden, in Millbrook, New York, where the hills and cup-shaped valleys honour the Chinese style, and in Percy Cane's pseudo-medieval tiltyard at Dartington, in Devon, which includes a Henry Moore nude at the top. More recently, landform – generally used as abstract hummocks or terraces on slopes, or as conical mounds in urban public spaces – has become fashionable among landscape architects. Kathryn Gustafson models her designs in clay in order to realize her ideas more precisely, and in America Peter Walker and Martha Schwartz have both used turf mounds to good effect.

Land art

In 1947 Isamu Noguchi drew up plans for the unrealized *Sculpture to be Seen From Mars*, a stylized face in the desert with a nose a mile long. Intended as a grimly apocalyptic 'memorial to man' (its earlier title), it was the precursor to an American art movement that emerged in the mid-1960s. Robert Smithson, Walter de Maria, Michael Heizer and Robert Morris were among the artists who began to explore ways of leaving the confines of the gallery and working on a large scale, using the landscape as a medium. These land artists had an ambivalent attitude towards the natural world, being alternately aggressive and nurturing, and seeking out wilderness or reclamation sites that could be manipulated for artistic ends.

One of Michael Heizer's most ambitious landforms was *Effigy Tumuli* (1985), which had a mystical aspect. Five huge earth mounds, sculpted as stylized, geometric animals, looked either primitive or extra-terrestrial – a common confusion, and one exploited by the crop-circle makers. Many land artists are preoccupied with making naked-eye observatories that echo ancient methodologies, including Charles Ross's *Star Axis*, near Santa Fe, where the North Star will be viewed up a stainless-steel tunnel. As visitors ascend, the orbit of Polaris changes size and the historical moment in time this represents is carved on each step. The ecological impulse is also strong in land art, not least because it is often the reason for a commission from a corporation or council with ugly landfills to explain away.

The idea behind Robert Smithson's most celebrated work, *Spiral Jetty* (1970), at Utah's Great Salt Lake, was to create a 'non-site'. His intention was to transcend both landscape and the traditional contexts for viewing art. As was observed, instead of putting a work of art on some land, Smithson put some land into a work of art. In Arizona, James Turrell's Roden Crater, an extinct volcano that he began excavating in 1977, is the most exciting landform project underway today, and is due to open to the public in 2011. The finished crater, moulded to a perfect circle, will contain fourteen skyspaces honed from the rock. Ironically, given the scale of the undertaking, Turrell is not interested in land, but light. The sky, not the earth, is his medium. There is no object, no image, no point of focus – just a succession of room spaces that reflect, refract or reveal expanses of sky. 'In the end,' Turrell says, 'what we are doing is gardening the sky.'

Turrell is not exactly a land artist; his skyspaces are laboratories where light can be experienced as an almost abstract effect. For most land artists, however, landscape is just another medium. Michael Heizer stated simply: 'I work outside because it is the only place where I can displace mass.' Smithson moved the concept on to embrace time and the way it takes on a physical presence in the landscape: 'The pastoral is outmoded. The gardens of history are being replaced by sites of time.' Whether it is presented as art or as a form of design, perhaps landform can provide an intimation of just this kind of immortality.

THE OFFICE OF JAMES BURNETT

SOLANA BEACH, CALIFORNIA / HOUSTON, TEXAS, USA

Elegant park design and glamorous private gardens, all conceived in the tradition of the Modernist conviction that 'gardens are for people'.

Boldness and simplicity are the watchwords at the Office of James Burnett (OJB), established in Houston in 1989, with a San Diego branch added in 2003. Elegant groundplans create frameworks for designs that incorporate tree-lined allées, raised rills and groves of trees, constituting a muscular yet subtle development of Modernism. The old functionalist creed remains strong: this company is exceptionally attuned to the needs of clients and potential users, constantly trying to imagine the different physical and psychological requirements of the people who are to use a given space.

One of OJB's most successful recent projects is the design for a landscape around the new Brochstein Pavilion at Rice University (2010), in Houston, Texas. The glass-walled cafeteria building, designed by Thomas Phifer & Partners, gave the university's central quadrangle an identity and a use, while OJB's remit was to encourage students to linger in the landscape. Set in a field of decomposed granite, a grove of forty-eight lacebark elms echoes the form of the building and helps organize the space between the pavilion and the adjacent library. Two low concrete fountains define the area underneath the canopy, and movable seating accommodates impromptu gatherings. Additional plantings of live oaks and improved pathways reinforce the existing frame-work of the quadrangle. The overall effect is akin to a Modernist landscape design, such as that created by Dan Kiley at the Miller House, in Indiana. There is an air of classical repose in these spaces, augmented here by the presence of a 'table' of water, recalling descriptions of banquets in Pliny's letters (during which plates were trans-ported to diners by a flowing rill) and the design of the 16th-century Villa Lante at Bagnaia, which, with its watery banqueting table, was itself inspired by Pliny.

01

03

04

01 A pebble-lined rill bisects the grove that
   surrounds the new Brochstein Pavilion
   at Rice University, in Houston, Texas.
02 The bold sweeps of the groundplan of
   The Park at Chicago's Lakeshore East
   development can be appreciated from
   the surrounding high-rise buildings.
03 The enormous scale of the plan is made
   even more appropriate by the site's
   context at the edge of Lake Michigan.
04 The level of detail in the specification
   of the paving aids orientation for park
   visitors.

The Park at Lakeshore East (2005) in Chicago, Illinois, is a 2.1-hectare (5.3-acre) urban landscape project that is the central amenity of a development in the city's Inner Loop. Overlooking the confluence of the Chicago River and Lake Michigan, the $4 billion redevelopment, 11.3-hectare (28-acre) in total, will, upon completion, include 4,950 residential units, 1,500 hotel rooms, 204,387m^2 (2.2 million sq ft) of commercial space, 71,535m^2 (770,000 sq ft) of retail space and an elementary school. Two sweeping promenades serve as the primary circulation routes across the site, with each featuring a series of fountain basins, seating areas and ornamental gardens. And serving as an extension of Field Street's axis, a Grand Stair offers a commanding view of the park and accommodates the 7.6m (25 ft) grade differential created by the city's three-tiered transit system. Additional amenities include a children's garden, a dog park and an event lawn.

05 A series of square pools double up as
benches and help create a focal area for
the Lakeshore East development, while
the park is in a phase of maturing.

OSSART & MAURIÈRES

PARIS, FRANCE

Planting duo who specialize in naturalistic yet effortlessly chic design, much of it now in Morocco and North Africa.

The distinctively Mediterranean sensibility of this duo, who have been based in Taroudant, Morocco, since 2003, has been influenced by the rammed-earth architecture of North Africa. Eric Ossart was formerly head gardener at the Chaumont festival, the pioneering venue for conceptualist landscape design; Arnaud Maurières, meanwhile, had been artistic director of the influential salon L'Art du Jardin, and founded the École Méditerranéenne des Jardins et du Paysage, in Grasse. In the late 1980s, the pair developed a type of urban planting – *le nouveau fleurissement* – for the city of Blois to replace the worn-out bedding schemes that were common at the time. Taking inspiration from meadows, farmhouse gardens and allotments, they formulated an exuberant vocabulary that soon found imitators all over France, and was also used for the gardens of the Cluny museum of medieval art in Paris.

Of the Tilsitt garden (2004), in Paris, Ossart and Maurières say: 'This one project unites our complete range of city-garden types: a large entry courtyard, two smaller ones, roof terraces and several long balconies. On the main roof, a prairie garden mixes grasses and tall perennials. Along the balconies, high, narrow zinc containers are planted with fig trees, roses and buddleias. A lower courtyard is shaded by hardy banana and palm trees for a very exotic effect. For the roof garden, we took inspiration from a work session in Chicago [at the university's school of architecture]. The shallow soil layer allowed on the roof would not accommodate the planting of trees, or even shrubs. We therefore took the great American prairies for our model, and used high grasses and brightly coloured wildflowers. Even the garden furniture was made from an American design to affirm the identity of the garden.'

01 The rooftop Tilsitt garden in the centre
   of Paris is a series of balconies and other
   outdoor spaces, where the planting theme
   was inspired by the American prairie model.

02-05 Of the Al Hossoun garden in Morocco,
the designers say: 'We divided the terrain
into numerous courtyards and gardens,
which alternate orchards and productive
spaces for good eating, which are regularly
watered, with dry gardens, experimental
botanical collections where we plant the
finds from arid parts of the globe like
Mexico or Yemen.'

05

The 6-hectare (15-acre) Al Hossoun garden (2005), a series of courtyards for a hotel at Taroudant, was an early experiment with rammed-earth architecture and the use of dry-climate plants that the pair had collected in Madagascar, Yemen and Mexico. Bedrooms, sitting rooms and hammams are ranged around what could be described as a labyrinthine botanical garden, with several possible entrances and exits in each space. There are three principal courtyards: a 'parterre' of roses and pennisetum grass, plus salad plants; a courtyard with a formal pool; and a sheltered sunken garden with exotic and tender plantings. There is also a garden of spiky, succulent agaves, euphorbia and cacti, while overall there is an emphasis on bright colour and edible plants. Pots, often empty, are sculpturally grouped.

At the Noria gardens (2000), near Uzès, in southern France, the starting point was a water-pumping system that belonged to an 18th-century manor house. The garden is closely integrated with the surrounding landscape. Each feature in the distant panorama connects with an axis of the garden: one path leads the eye towards Montaigu; a line of cypresses is orientated towards a hill town; and an orchard frames the distant fields. But the overriding aesthetic is Moorish–Andalucian. A grove of pomegranate trees, underplanted with iris, agapanthus and anenomes, flanks a long pool connected to a rill, echoing the work of Luis Barragán. The rill defines an avenue edged with cypress, intermingled with fragrant flowering shrubs: philadelphus, roses and honeysuckle. Multi-stemmed fig trees and the local redbud (*Cercis siliquastrum*) form a canopy for summer shade. This walk ends in a formal 'cloister', shaded by canopies of *Celtis australis*, a common tree in the region. Beyond lies a rose parterre, a cherry orchard and a truffle wood of oak and hazelnuts. Certain Mediterranean themes have been 'borrowed' for the garden, but as the designers observe: 'This is a Mediterranean without the sea, a world of earth and wind, of farming and irrigation, of fresh running water, of fruit swollen with sugar and sun, and fragrant flowers.'

06-08 A modern take on the Andalucian pool garden, near Uzès, France. The pool is surrounded by pomegranate trees, while the avenue is defined by a rill filled with the scent of flowering shrubs. The contemporary chairs in concrete were designed by Pierre Baey.

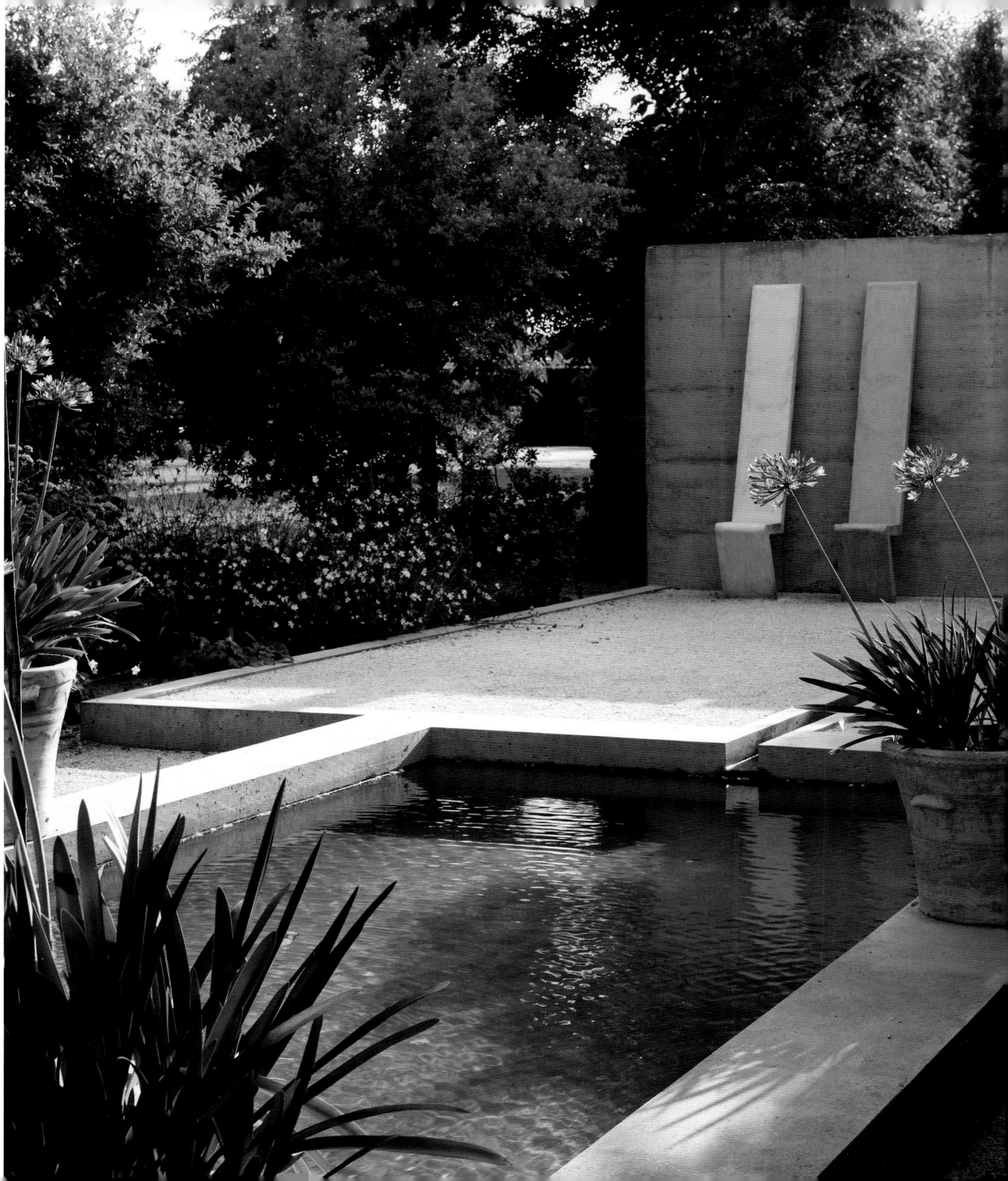

PIET OUDOLF

HUMMELO, NETHERLANDS

Pioneer of the New Perennials school of naturalistic planting design,
here is a garden designer with a truly international reputation.

An international profile is a rare thing among even the most accomplished garden designers, but plantsman Piet Oudolf has gained just that as the leader of the New Perennials movement in planting design. He has been fêted in England for at least the past decade, with high-profile projects including Pensthorpe Nature Reserve (2000), in Norfolk, a long, double border at the Royal Horticultural Society's garden at Wisley, Surrey (2002), and most recently, a new extravaganza at Scampston Hall, in Yorkshire. His skills have now been noted by American designers, and his work can be seen at Battery Park and the new High Line park, both in Lower Manhattan, and at the Lurie Garden in Chicago's Millennium Park.

Oudolf began his gardening career at the age of twenty-five, after deciding against going into the family restaurant business. His main influences were Karl Foerster, who pioneered the naturalistic look in Germany's public parks, and Mien Ruys, a Dutchwoman who blended planting skill with innovative Modernist structure. At his own garden at Hummelo, near Arnhem, Oudolf developed a planting style that was wholly dependent on the structure and form of perennial plants, particularly grasses. It is a more complex, condensed, sculptural and nuanced version of the kind of work that was being done in Germany and Holland in the post-war years. By the mid-1990s the style had been given the 'New Perennials' tag, and since then it has inspired numerous disciples in Holland, France, Germany and Britain.

Oudolf had already been making gardens for a select group of British clients, but burst into public consciousness courtesy of a series of books published at the turn of the Millennium, which described how to create naturalistic gardens using a palette of

01 The walled garden at Scampston Hall is one
of the best places to see Oudolf's planting
style as it matures and grows. Drifts
and clumps of key perennials are artfully
repeated within a severe hedged structure.

grasses and tall perennials. The most successful of these was *Designing with Plants* (1999), written in collaboration with Noël Kingsbury (see p. 268). Having designed gardens at Pensthorpe Nature Reserve and RHS Wisley, the Royal Horticultural Society's endorsement, though controversial at the time, reflected the impact of the New Perennials style. Today, many British gardens betray Oudolf's influence to some degree. He has persuaded gardeners to make grasses and taller perennials a key feature of the ornamental garden, which is now more often planted for form and structure than for colour. Shrubs, which were beginning to decline in popularity in the 1980s, have been increasingly replaced by grasses and other bulky plants as structural subjects – much to the chagrin of some traditional plantsmen.

03

04

02-04 At Scampston Hall, Oudolf has utilized
      single-species plantings of grasses in
      pattern beds and areas of topiary shapes to
      contrast with the richness and complexity
      of his perennials plantings elsewhere.

07

05-07 The Pensthorpe Nature Reserve in Norfolk
was one of Oudolf's first major commissions
in the UK. It exhibits his signature
method of planting in naturalistic drifts,
complemented by bursts of colour and
striking plant forms.

What is revolutionary about Oudolf's approach is the way he claims to disregard colour entirely when planning borders. He argues: 'The form and structure of plants is more intrinsic to them than colour, and gardeners should be paying it more attention. Flower colour is with us for a relatively short season, compared with the shape of the plant – with perennials from spring until winter. If you want to create plantings that evoke nature and provide a long-lasting season of interest, then you should concentrate on learning about plant form, and think of colour only as an exciting extra.' In this view, there is no such thing as a 'wrong' or bad-taste colour combination. All of this is heresy to the English gardening tradition and its devotees around the world. Painterly colour-theming, in the Gertrude Jekyll manner, has been the bedrock of herbaceous gardening throughout the 20th century, and it has remained important during the various mutations of the herbaceous border – from the mid-century cottagey, pastel-coloured effusions to the 'tapestry' approach that emerged in the 1980s.

But for Oudolf, there is more than enough interest in swaying drifts of grasses such as stipa, miscanthus and molinia, offset by sculptural notes from the spires of digitalis, verbascum, persicaria and salvias, or the fluffy plumes of filipendula or thalictrum. It is the shape of the plant that matters, and so he creates repetition and rhythm by using groups of daisy forms (rudbeckias, echinacea, asters and inulas) or flat-capped umbellifers such as sedum, angelica, eupatorium and achillea. Dead plants are left in situ, and Oudolf encourages gardeners not only to appreciate the charms of wilting seedheads (which is easy enough), but also to revel in the various brown tones of dead – and sometimes soggy – leaves.

08-11 The High Line in New York is a disused aerial
railway line that is being transformed into
an elevated park that runs through the
Meatpacking District on the Lower West Side.
Oudolf worked with landscape designers Field
Operations to create various discrete planting
zones, which meld with the remains of the
railway to create a postindustrial frisson
and a new tourist attraction.

11

DAN PEARSON

LONDON, ENGLAND

Deep-thinking, emotionally engaged designer who fuses a modern vision with an acute sensitivity to natural landscapes.

In the late 1980s and '90s, while most British garden designers remained entranced by the Arts and Crafts traditions of herbaceous planting, Dan Pearson was almost alone in advocating a more modern approach. Via a string of private gardens and a succession of television series, he promoted the idea of a garden that united a love of plants and the natural world with a kind of stylish functionalism that appealed to garden owners under the age of forty. Towards the end of the 1990s, this attitude had gone mainstream, and Pearson was hailed as an innovator ahead of his time, just as John Brookes had been in the 1960s. If anything, however, Pearson's work has become more naturalistic over the years, testament to his credentials as a plantsman, with a Kew training and years of experience with plant communities in the wild all over the world. One of Pearson's formative influences was Beth Chatto, whose garden in Essex demonstrates the way a garden's style can reflect the habits of self-supporting communities of plants as they thrive in nature. To this, Pearson adds a deep appreciation of a site's sense of place, which he aims to enhance and reflect with his designs.

Pearson's gardens are usually based on strong, clear structural bones, both in terms of elegant curves in the hard landscape and groundplan, and in a liking for horticultural features such as lines of pleached trees or clipped yew hedges in bulbous form. A sculpted spatial quality resounds through the work; of principal importance, he says, are the 'relationships between spaces and the creation of holistic environments with distinctive moods'. In recent commissions, Pearson has explored an ever more naturalistic feel, with an emphasis on wildflower plantings with mown paths meandering through them, plantings of native trees, subtle turf landforms, and the

01 The landformed area of the Tokachi
Millennium Forest, on the island of Hokkaido,
Japan, serves as a transition zone for visitors
to the site, and as a way of enticing them
further into the natural landscape.
02 The entrance walk is flanked by massed
plantings of perennials to create an
exciting prelude to the visit.

03

04

05

decorative possibilities of traditional walling. At Pearson's most significant long-term project, Home Farm in Northamptonshire, it was the surrounding agricultural landscape of the ancient ridge-and-furrow fields that provided the inspiration. In recent years, his practice has expanded internationally, with projects in Italy, the USA and Japan, where he is collaborating with Conran & Partners by creating fourteen ambitious roof gardens for the Roppongi Hills housing development in Tokyo.

The Tokachi Millennium Forest (2008), located on the Japanese island of Hokkaido, is being developed as an educational public park, sustainable for one thousand years. It is the brainchild of entrepreneur Mitsushige Hayashi, who acquired the land with a view to offsetting the carbon footprint of his newspaper business. Pearson is collaborating with Takano Landscape Planning on the creation of a river walk, a forest trail, wild meadowland, a farm garden, an ornamental garden, and the integration of a hotel complex, restaurant, visitor centre and car parking. The entrance walk meanders through a well-managed woodland of wild flowers to the edge of a stream, over which zig-zags a raised timber path. Glimpses of livestock in the open fields add a pastoral quality. Spring begins with white skunk cabbage, marsh marigold and anemones. While the ground is still relatively bare there are sheets of trillium, as candelabra primulas and astilbe trace the moist hollows. Veratrum, arisaema, giant angelicas and aruncus follow, and pale-green cardiocrinums, scented day lilies, asters and *Iris sanguinea* grow on the fringes. A giant, sinuous earthwork at the base of the foothills grounds the visitor centre and café, forming a shield between the cultivated garden areas and the surrounding landscape. After this landform environment,

03–06 There are many moods to discover at the Tokachi Millennium Forest. A key tenet of Pearson's work is the idea of honouring the sense of place in a landscape by observing and then replicating or complementing natural plant communities.

visitors are enticed further by massed colour-themed ribbon plantings of native perennials, which spill over the fields and into the woodland.

For a private garden on the island of Guernsey (2006), in the English Channel, Pearson introduced a series of terraces, which refer to local contour lines, in place of the existing, and rather claustrophobic, garden spaces. Some of the terraces are laid to grass, providing access to the upper levels of the site, while others are planted profusely with ornamental perennials. The south-facing pool terrace to the east of the property forms the hub of the garden, and was designed for inside–outside living with an internal swimming pool that connects visually with an external pond. 'One of the main challenges of this site is that the sense of place is influenced both by Guernsey's specific microclimate and the surrounding pastoral farmland,' Pearson says. 'So while we ensured that the planting made the most of the mild climate, it was also integrated into the local landscape. The stonework on Guernsey is particular to the island and we used local stone and stone workers for all of the hard landscaping.'

At Broughton Hall business park (2002), in Yorkshire, Pearson landscaped the 0.8-hectare (2-acre) walled garden around a new, glass-walled cafeteria pavilion. Yew buttress hedges form divisions within the large open site, breaking up the space and forming distinct enclosed areas that serve to contain soft, massed naturalistic perennial plantings. The other project illustrated here is a private garden in Oxfordshire (2005), where Pearson contributed a sculptural landform in the shape of a mound and basin, which plays on the idea of full versus empty, while also referring to the occupation of one of the clients as a potter.

07-10 For this private garden on Guernsey, a series of terraces behind the house follow the contour lines of the landscape. The drystone walling by local craftsmen honours the vernacular traditions of the area.

11

12

11 At Broughton Hall business park in Yorkshire, Pearson redesigned a Victorian walled garden for office workers, so that it has become a place of secret walks and hidden spaces, defined by massed plantings of perennials.
12 Pearson's interest in landform is also expressed on a smaller scale at this private garden in Oxfordshire, which makes reference to the client's occupation as a ceramicist.

PÉNA & PEÑA PAYSAGES

PARIS, FRANCE

Exciting and original yet highly formalized landscape design,
most of it in the public sphere.

Christine and Michel Péna have been working as landscape architects since 1984, specializing in public squares and parks, and have achieved a substantial body of work. They established Péna & Peña Paysages in 2004 and currently employ a team of fourteen architects, engineers and landscape architects.

Michel Péna's most celebrated work to date, designed in collaboration with François Brun, is the Jardin Atlantique (1997), located on the 3.4-hectare (8.4-acre) roofspace of the Montparnasse railway station in Paris's 15th arrondissement. This vast roof garden comes as a considerable surprise to anyone who comes across it (quite often rail passengers awaiting their trains). The name of the park refers to the high-speed trains that depart from this station for the Atlantic coast in northern France. This central theme informs every aspect of the garden's design, bringing something of the coastal drama of Brittany to an intensely urban space.

Faced with a great slab of concrete and little planting depth with which to work, the designers decided to defy expectations and create a garden with a 'theatrical aesthetic', replete with ambitious water features and full-sized trees. The mature trees were planted directly above the steel columns that hold up the station's roof, while the central water feature was realized in a shallow metal basin. The tree specification stipulated that one side of the garden be planted with American tree species and the other with European species, to bolster the 'Atlantic' theme. There are tennis courts, children's play areas, lawns, enclosed garden rooms and a boardwalk, as well as enough seating for nearly five hundred people at any one time (though it has to be said that this hidden garden is usually almost deserted). The fountain, named 'The Island of

01-04 The Jardin Atlantique on the rooftop of Gare Montparnasse evokes the Atlantic Ocean in all its many guises, from the coastal regions of Brittany to the ocean's history as a space of exploration. Boardwalks and mature trees map out a variety of different spaces, providing a sense of privacy and transcendence in the middle of Paris.

05

05 A plan of Le Jardin du Couchant, one of three public gardens designed for the roofspace of the underground station at Vincennes, outside Paris.
06 Le Jardin du Levant, which incorporates amorphous island beds filled with grasses and pine trees.
07 The straight, central walkway at the third garden, Le Jardin du Midi.

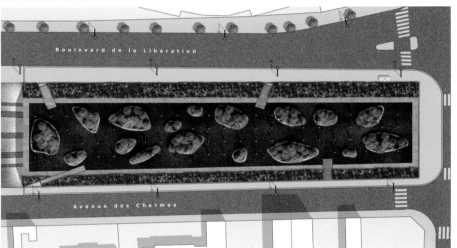

06

08 Le Jardin du Couchant features a central boardwalk lined with orange poles, some of which support single chairs.
09 The walkway at Le Jardin du Midi is covered with a thin film of water, which rises to a grand metal staircase.
10 The vivid blue surface at Le Jardin du Levant.

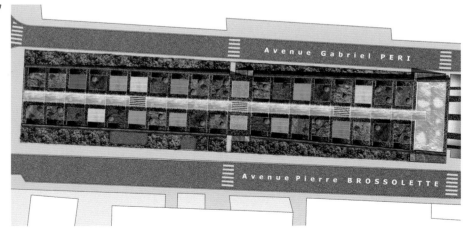

07

08

09

10

11

12

13

14

11-14 At Le Serre d'Aubrias, in the Cévennes region, the duo envisaged a realignment, developing over several decades, between a farmhouse and its surrounding terraces and pool.

Hesperides', contains an oversized thermometer, a rain gauge, a weather vane and an anemometer, which measures wind speed. Other parts of the garden have been given lyrical names such as 'The Isle of the Blessed'.

The firm collaborated on another railway project, this time at Vincennes, in the suburbs of Paris (2008). Here, three linear parks, divided by roads, were designed for the roof of the underground station. Le Jardin du Couchant is abundantly planted and contains a central boardwalk that runs the length of the park, punctuated by wooden decks or 'nests'. These areas contain children's play equipment and mist machines, while chairs suspended on metal masts are scattered along the main path. Le Jardin du Levant features an all-over blue artificial surface, in which island beds are planted with grasses, pines and other hardy plants. The aesthetic of bright-orange wooden poles is carried over from Le Jardin du Couchant, here doubling up as play equipment and lighting poles. There is plenty of seating, along with a raised walkway that surrounds the space. The third garden is Le Jardin du Midi, which features, as the designers put it, 'a grand staircase of water and stone that leads to heaven' at one end. The garden gradually rises to the foot of the staircase, delineated by a long, central walkway in black granite that is covered with a thin film of water. Its sobriety is offset by the slabs of bright colours that accompany the walker in this dramatic space.

At Le Serre d'Aubrias (ongoing), in the Cévennes region of south-central France, the designers wished to relate the architecture of the existing ancient farmhouse to its terraces, while also paying due respect to the massive scale of the surrounding landscape. The result is a design that is intended to realize itself only over a period of at least twenty years. The terraces have been planted with a range of flora that is naturally found in this area, while the pool is intended to provide a landscape linkage between the temporal and celestial worlds.

PLANERGRUPPE OBERHAUSEN

OBERHAUSEN, GERMANY

Thoughtful, austerely elegant designs from
this highly professional practice.

Founded in 1973, Planergruppe Oberhausen is a collaborative company led by Ulrike Beuter and Harald Fritz, supported by six other landscape architects. Its position in the middle of the densely populated and industrial Ruhr-Emscher region of Germany means that it has developed a particularly pragmatic attitude to open space and urban planning. 'The character of a place has to do with the people who inhabit it,' they say. 'Therefore, we give extensive consideration to the surroundings and established structures. Thus the design of open spaces is also always urban planning.' The curt mission statement continues: 'Designing landscapes means making space tangible. To sharpen the viewer's perception of the specific characteristics of a place, we make restrained but conscious use of architectural elements and materials. We do not produce striking event landscapes, but feel our way into the language of the existing elements. We do not conjure up lovely natural landscapes, but set up frameworks that draw attention to the existing qualities of a landscape.'

At the former Zollverein coal mine and coking plant in Essen, the firm is implementing a postindustrial design covering some 80 hectares (198 acres), due to be completed in 2012. Coal was first mined here in 1851, but when activity ceased in 1993 the owners were ready to demolish the impressive range of buildings, towers and equipment at the site, which was subsequently awarded World Heritage Site status and protected in perpetuity. The park's curators note that the design of the Zollverein coal mine was 'architecturally rooted in the style of *Neue Sachlichkeit* (new objectivity): strong, symmetrical and geometric lines, individual cubic buildings in a correspondingly strict arrangement'. Four of the five shaft sites have been preserved, along with

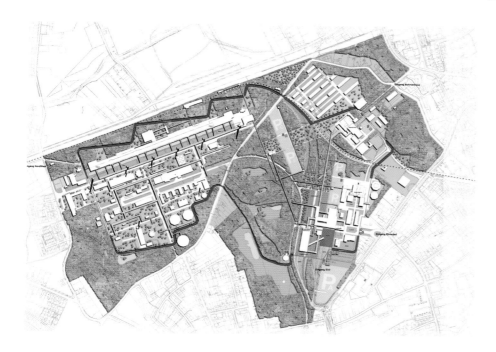

01-04 This former coal mine and coking plant has been remodelled as a centre of creativity for the region, principally through the imaginative siting and realization of footpaths and cycleways.

the underground equipment, coking plant, spoil tips, transport sites and housing estates. Architect Rem Koolhaas produced a masterplan for Zollverein in 2002, and since then the site has been energetically developed as a cultural hub for the local community, with a new architectural school, ice rink, swimming pool and museum. Perhaps surprisingly, the landscape was the final element to be considered.

When the plant closed in 1993, artists and other creatives were quickly allowed to colonize the buildings while nature – birch trees, shrubs, ferns and moss – began to take over the fenced-off landscape. Later, the landscape was gradually opened up and paths were laid, and it was used as a setting for granite sculpture by Ulrich Rückriem. In 2005 the firm won a competition alongside art practices, lighting designers and communications specialists to work on the landscape. The rationale was to capitalize on what remained on site and allow for a wide range of interpretations of any particular feature, so that it could be appreciated by tourists and locals alike over a long period. The entrances to the park are to be marked by six pavilions containing artworks curated by the Rotterdam art collective, Observatorium. Elsewhere, three-dimensional steel models of the park will help with visitor orientation. Planergruppe Oberhausen will also be involved in converting the trackways in the park to footpaths, and adding grassy berms and garden spaces within the birch woodland. Finally, a 4km- (2.5 mile-) perimeter walkway and cycle track will be constructed, taking visitors through a variety of environments, from the stony pits near the coking plant to wooded groves on higher ground.

POLA

BERLIN, GERMANY

Unusual forms utilized on a city-square scale characterize this fearless public-landscape practice.

Pola stands for 'poetic landscapes', and founder Jörg Michel exhibits a disarmingly populist attitude: 'Beauty simply is a source of happiness. Pola makes people happy by designing beautiful places.' Digging a little deeper, the firm emerges as a company with a distinctly conceptualist streak: 'We focus our design on the history and the sense of the places we work on. As every place has its own stories, we play with them, interpret them and transform them into new, poetic landscapes.' In terms of form, this means strikingly amorphous or linear groundplans, which are filled with incident and discrete spaces that have 'something to say'. Michel continues: 'We believe that form does not necessarily follow function. We create from a basis of emotion and sensitivity in order to interact with visitors.'

Pola's design for the City Balcony in Hangzhou, China, is based on the notion of reintegrating the city with its river, the Qian Tang, which was previously ignored – as rivers often are – in the urban planning of the area. To help redress this, a 500m- (1,640 ft-) long shopping complex was constructed adjacent to the river, with a roofspace and promenades some 80m (262 ft) above the surface of the water. Pola created a viewing 'balcony', both as a means of appreciating the river and as an outdoor promenade and park space for people using the mall. Once a year, the river becomes swollen and exhibits unusual and dramatic wave patterns, and the new balcony allows the city's residents to see this happening. Pola's intention was to create a sense of seamless transition between inside and out with their design – perhaps not an original ambition among landscape architects, but potentially more of a reality in the case of a building that was designed at the same time as its landscape spaces.

01 The City Balcony in Hangzhou, China, is a 'park-promenade' on the roof of a new shopping mall, which provides dramatic views of the Qian Tang River, courtesy of raised walkways.

01

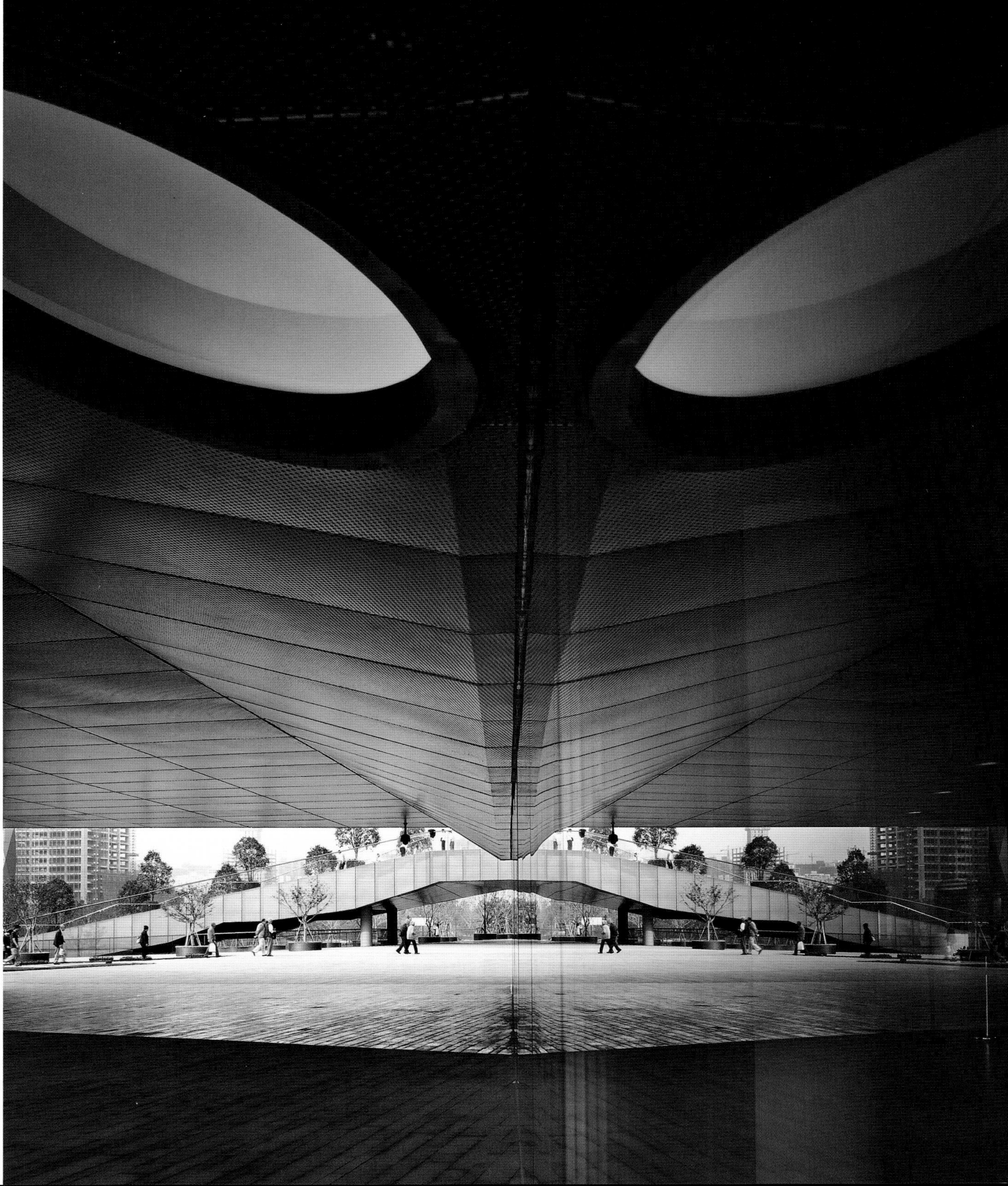

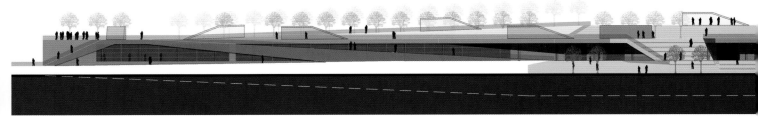

03

04

'The exchange between light and shadow creates a meandering structure of wood, grass and stone along the surface of the promenade,' Michel says. 'Promenade and landscape merge together. The structure of the landscape promenade expresses the flow of the Qian Tang River and its play with the tides.' What Michel means by this last statement is the way the patterning of the ground surfaces in the City Balcony echoes, or 'quotes' (to use his word), the kinds of pattern that can be discerned on beaches or at river edges, when the tide has receded or is receding. Over one thousand newly planted trees, in loose groupings, define the new 'park-promenade'; species include *Cinnamomum camphora*, *Magnolia grandiflora* and yew.

Pola is a relatively young company that is currently going through the usual period – for ambitious firms – of entering competitions in order to make a name and secure commissions. In 2010 Pola won an international competition for the design of two new parks covering the federal Autobahn at Hamburg-Stellingen/Schnelsen.

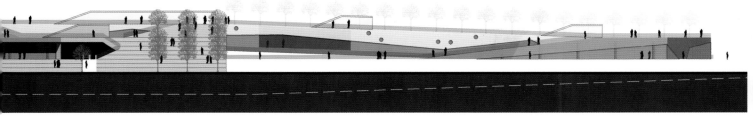

05

02-05 The landscape aesthetic was inspired by the
     patterns made on sand or mud by receding
     tidal waters. Pola extended this motif
     across the entirety of the design, while
     tree plantings were intended to create
     a 'soft haze' that enhances the 'poetic'
     atmosphere of the place.

PATRIZIA POZZI

MILAN, ITALY

A true original, this designer has worked in many styles and mediums, but always makes the space her own.

Having trained as a landscape architect and horticulturist in Genoa and Milan, qualifying in 1987, Patrizia Pozzi has worked for a variety of private and public clients – almost always in Italy – creating gardens and landscape spaces that straddle the divide between art and garden. Her work is distinguished by its strong artistic identity and her own personality as an artist. It frequently exhibits an aesthetic of bold patterning, together with the white-rendered walls and green lawns familiar from the Modernist vocabulary, though Pozzi's spatial arrangements tend to be more complex than they would be in a traditional Modernist genre.

Pozzi sums up her own attitude in this way: 'In every project I like to combine and connect the world of nature and the world of daily life. Through an ironic and sensitive approach, I always try to catch the peculiarities of a site, operating so that I am both respecting and evaluating the intrinsic traits of the place. It is essential to feel and to know the site's context: to breathe the air; to feel the wind; to smell the scents; to see the colours. My personal desires always come together with this knowledge. Sometimes I really play with nature: a house or tower might be shaped like a shell; a bench like a hedge; a seat like a piece of coral; or a glass house like a giant egg.'

Four Season Parterre (2003) was created for the roofspace of a new L'Oréal building in Milan, where only a very little weight was possible because of the presence of a parking garage beneath. Pozzi decided to selectively quote an 18th-century Italian parterre design as the template for the space, as a way of reacting against the scale of the refurbished building and its dense urban surroundings. Paths of yellow gravel (Verona marble) intersect with panels of lawn and splashes of floral colour that change with

01-04 The roofspace of the L'Oréal building in Milan is based on an Italian parterre design from the 18th century. The pattern is picked out in gravel and grass; different colour notes are provided by seasonal plantings of annual flowers and other plants.

01 02 03

04

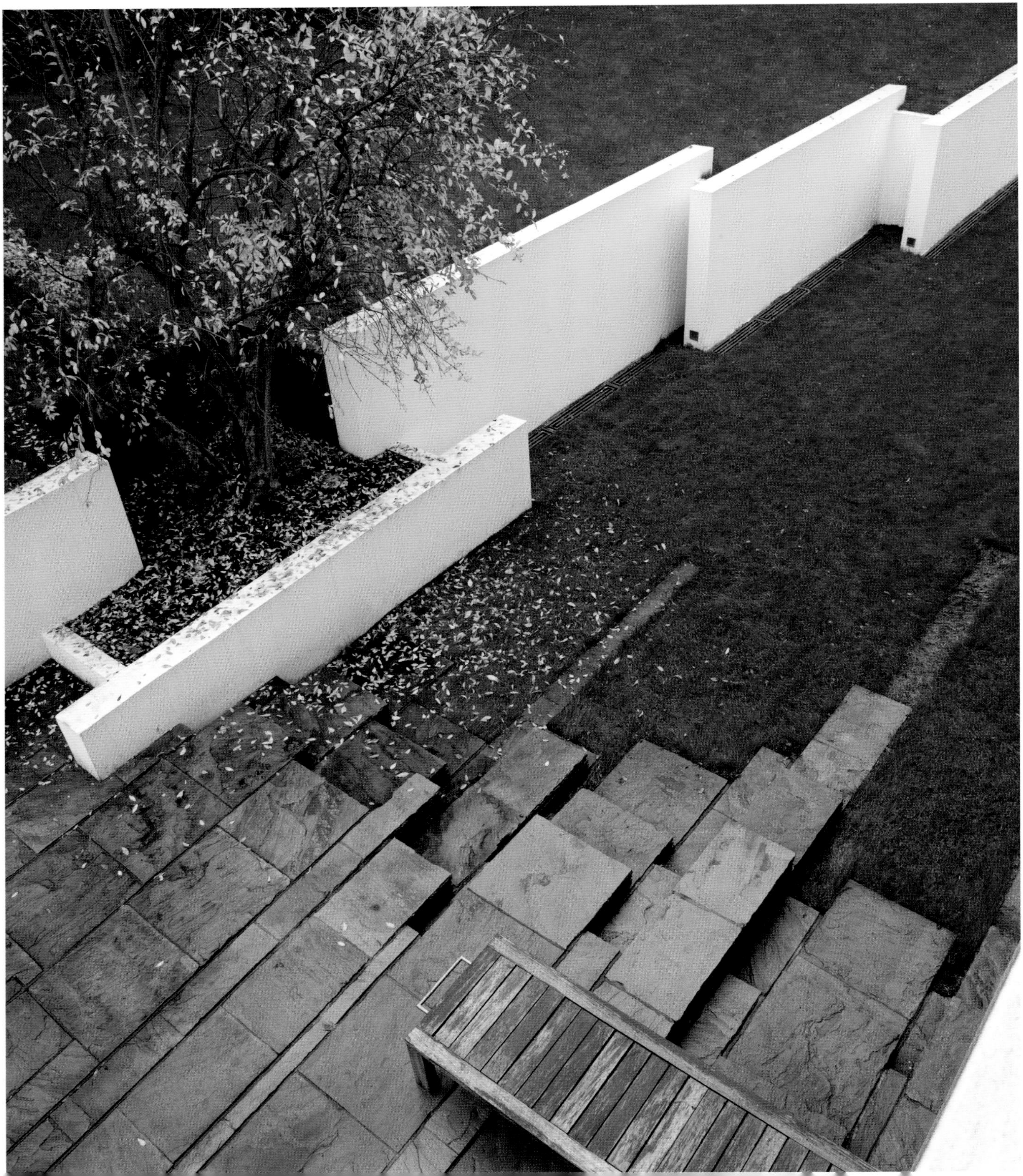

05-07 For a private residence in the Italian town of Carnate, Pozzi extended the Modernist appearance of the house into the garden by means of white-rendered linear walls that act as sculptural interventions.

the seasons: *Erica vulgaris* in autumn, *Viola cornuta* in winter, *Primula vulgaris* in spring and Impatiens 'New Guinea' in summer. Office workers are allowed to walk upon any part of the parterre.

At a private garden in Carnate (2001), in the Lombardy region of Italy, about 25km (15.5 miles) north-east of Milan, Pozzi was faced with an unusual triangular space, which was cluttered with decorative detritus when she arrived. Much of this was removed, and the garden's integrity restored and enhanced by additions from Pozzi, who renovated both house and garden at the same time. The white-walled Modernist aesthetic of the building was extended into the garden by the use of linear walls, envisaged in an essentially sculptural manner, and by small ranges of steps. Existing hedges were reshaped and pruned and an artificial boxwood couch was added to create an ironic note. Near the house is a rectangular pool and covered dining area, while at the far end of the garden is a monumental wall-like abstract sculpture, somewhat reminiscent of the enlarged Ben Nicholson relief sculpture used by Geoffrey Jellicoe for his iconic design at Sutton Place, near Guildford in Surrey. Pozzi says that the process of rethinking the design of this garden 'enabled us to discover the intrinsically beautiful balances and geometrical effects of the space'.

06

07

THE FUTURE OF LANDSCAPE DESIGN: FORUM ONE

A selection of the world's most influential landscape and garden designers and critics were asked to respond briefly to the following simple question: 'What are the greatest opportunities and challenges facing landscape designers in the early 21st century?'

Richard Weller

There are now around 6.5 billion people on earth, a figure expected to rise to 9.5 billion by mid-century, before stabilizing soon thereafter. Why? Because even though you'd expect cities to incubate people, they actually don't: cities put a dampener on reproduction rates. As the world's population comes to live in predominantly urban settings, the human race will, for the first time since the agricultural revolution, stabilize numerically. What does continue to increase in cities, however, is expectation of 'quality of life'. This, of course, has major environmental consequences. The main issue facing landscape designers this century will therefore be whether the earth can support so many people, and whether we can design not only sustainable, but equitable systems of food, water and energy for them.

Of course, humans exhibit rat-like cunning and will survive. But survival at species level is not what this dilemma is about. What it is now about is whether 9.5 billion of us can enjoy a certain quality of life – the quality of life that Western modernity promised. Currently, a billion people are malnourished, and it is predicted that two billion will not have access to potable water by 2050. Resource wars will break out, and a diaspora of climate-change refugees will be on the move to higher ground. And landscape architects will continue to make water gardens for the rich, in the Roman ruins of the future. In order to feed 9.5 billion people without cutting down any more forests, we will need to radically increase the yield from global agricultural landscapes. These are currently landscapes shaped by the black magic of the industrial revolution: fossil fuels. For a mere $80, the energy of one barrel of oil equals eleven years of manual work with a shovel. There is dignity in digging, but not that much.

Whether our new energy is predominantly nuclear and our crops genetically engineered or otherwise, one thing is for sure: the world's landscapes will become more, not less, an expression of technology. Landscape architects who cherish images of Arcadia in their hearts are profoundly mistaken. The great challenge will be how to engineer those landscapes, and in most cases retrofit them so they are more resilient. Monocultures are not resilient. As technology frees people from a peasant existence, they move to the cities. Like the vast agricultural landscapes upon which they depend, cities, too, will need to be reconstructed as living ecologies, not as wasteful, destructive machines for which 'nature' was merely a pleasant backdrop.

Nature is the new machine. Landscape architects will need to understand its structure, not its surface. McHarg was wrong. McHarg was right.

Noël Kingsbury

Much of the future of designed landscapes inevitably lies in the emerging economies. The worst-case scenario is a spread of 'green concrete' accompanying the bland, lowest-common-denominator steel-and-glass boxes of a globalized architectural profession. Militating against this, however, is the fact that the relationship between climate and planting inevitably forces a stronger sense of linkage between place and design.

There is a huge range of variation in landscape's cultural capital in emerging countries, and a range of culturally based attitudes towards public space, which often reflects deeper attitudes towards social, ethnic and gender divisions. Designed landscapes are above all a public good, something we all benefit from; there is something profoundly democratic about public space. The degree to which a society invests in public space is, of course, largely politically determined and closely related to other investments in public goods, although the strength of civil society can also be a factor. The ideal would be a Roberto Burle Marx in every emerging country, someone who can make a break with colonial traditions, introduce native flora into designs, celebrate regional distinctiveness and, above all, develop a new and appropriate national style – and achieve all of this with flair and charisma.

Martha Schwartz

'Pluses'

+ The profession of landscape architecture will continue to expand and increase its creative leadership by means of an expanding freedom of expression. It will function as an increasingly rich laboratory for research and exploration in diverse areas.
+ Landscape architecture will increase in its leadership role in planning cities and regions. Landscape architects are more and more often being asked first to the planning table to ensure that natural systems and the integration of open spaces within cities are defined in advance of architectural intervention.
+ The creative role of landscape architects as informed generalists and creatives will only increase as we deal with the exponential growth of information available to us as designers. The role of synthetic thinkers has emerged in response to this chaos of information, since the challenge is to integrate and create hierarchies out of this chaos, generating planning strategies and, ultimately, an aesthetic strategy.
+ The profession of landscape architecture will become more active as it becomes

apparent that densification is the holy grail of global sustainability. Our profession's importance with regard to sustainability becomes most vivid when dealing with the urban scale of landscape operations, where it is now understood that public-realm landscape is fundamental to the creation of healthy cities. Thus, the role of the urban landscape and its greater role in global sustainability will become more generally understood and appreciated.

+ The idea of 'landscape urbanism' is so general that it will inevitably fade in fashionable discourse. But the power of this idea will be exercised through the profession of landscape architecture, not just architecture. Landscape urbanism is not an object-based idea; it is a broader concept that is salient to the integration of ecological systems as they apply to the 'systems' of human habitation. Such systems require integrated thought and cross-boundary professionalism. It is an issue that cannot be resolved by the creation of buildings, but instead must integrate the many systems that underpin human activities, which are all embedded in and on the landscape. Landscape architects will be the professional enablers in the creation of cities that people 'choose' to live in – and if they do not have the luxury of choosing, can at least enjoy a decent quality of life.

+ The profession of landscape architecture is becoming a more attractive profession for artists, scientists and thought-leaders.

+ Boundaries between the design professions, including the most contentious boundary between fine art and design, will continue to be blurred. The design / art / technology / information silos present so many creative opportunities that the old-guard professional distinctions will not be able to hold back cross-boundary thinking and making.

'Minuses'

- Education in landscape design is currently in danger of foregoing less sexy skill sets: drawing by hand; learning to grade so as to be able to create nuanced forms, while at the same time understanding that landscapes must be scaled in relation to people; and learning how to use plants to create space and experience. These are fundamental skills for landscape architects that are not taught in any other discipline. As a profession, we must stay true to our roots while expanding our scope.

- The diminished emphasis on hand-drawing is a particular area of concern. Drawing is a powerful tool, for it can teach students How To See. It is also a way of thinking, something that is now better understood by scientific researchers, but not by most educators. Our ability to teach design is greatly reduced without this prime tool for teaching students to evaluate and analyse what they are seeing, and why things look as they do. This may lead to a profession that can strategize brilliantly, but cannot design spaces that are meaningful to the people who use them. This would, in fact, be the least 'sustainable' strategy of all, for people must have an emotional connection to spaces for them to become places that will be sustained. Computer design and illustration removes the designer from scale, which is the most important element in the creation of successful places and spaces for people. The form may be interesting, but without attention to scale, these interesting forms are doomed as functioning places for people to use and enjoy.

- We are becoming unable and/or unwilling to defend or define 'design' as it affects 'sustainability'. We must remember that people are part of nature, and are not separated from it.
- We must continue to hone our own individual voices as practitioners, lest we be swallowed by the all-encompassing, one-stop-shop behemoths that have recently evolved as business models in the profession of landscape architecture. Although these huge, multi-service practices can superficially appear to be convenient for clients, the quality of design is diminished because art and design are not comfortable business partners. We must continue to value our ability as designers to bring delight, surprise, beauty and meaning to a particular site. We must continue to communicate by means of our feelings if we are to make a difference to the quality of life for many people.

Gilles Clément

Up until the early 21st century, professional designers have responded to both public and private commissions by developing essentially just one area of competence: the composition of unbuilt space. The successful completion of this task – which sometimes justifies the term 'landscape architecture' – can extend even to details such as the designing of objects, with a view to creating a single harmonious whole, a unique style. Sometimes, too, the professional may have to answer certain questions that are usually put to a gardener; the designer must foresee the production of fruit and vegetables, for example, but above all must imagine a programme that is sustainable through time.

Today, for reasons linked to our growing ecological awareness of species-fragility everywhere on the planet, and of the ecological limits of the living world, the designer-gardener takes on an another mission, which may be completely unexpected: the protection of life. The designer is no longer simply an architect of space, but becomes the overseer of all forms of life that exist in each project, and even of those that may come by chance to take shelter on the site that is being transformed. Tomorrow's designers will still exercise their professional talents in the domain of organizing space, and still know how to handle the smallest details. But above all, they will know how to work with living species developing through time. It will be necessary to refine techniques of ecological management, and this will probably give rise to new areas of expertise for landscape designers. Specialists in the supervision of site evolution will regularly be awarded contracts, something as yet unheard of in the profession.

Bernard Tschumi
'Global versus Local'
Today, globalization means that areas formerly only moderately touched by worldwide financial trends are subject to unprecedented economic acceleration. New infrastructures and cities seem to appear almost overnight, while international architects are asked to intervene, sometimes after three-week competitions, in areas and cultures they often know little about. While the incongruous insertion of architectural signatures into alien environments may rightfully be questioned, these interventions can also be considered an inevitable part of the import and export of cultures over the ages. How should architects or landscape architects intervene in these worldwide cultures – by repeating an egotistical individual style, or by searching for an elusive communion, caught between pastiche and nostalgia, with mutating local cultures? Or is there another way?

When we started our design for our Elliptic City for forty thousand inhabitants near Santo Domingo, it was clear to us that we were to design a landscape before we could begin to conceive of individual buildings. Our intent was to conceive a full landscape strategy that would govern the future development of the town, its offices, housing, schools, hotels, hospitals and other public amenities. Elliptic City is based on a real context (the untouched forest near the ocean), an abstract concept (a proposed archipelago of elliptical building areas), and an active content (the uses and activities of the town). A global contemporary approach for the inside of each of the landscape 'islands' in the forest, together with a local sensibility for their surroundings, was our general strategy for the town.

Claude Cormier

More than any other design profession, landscape architecture elevates the notion of sustainability. What is needed, however, is the assertion of an ecological aesthetic through a critical practice that is based on solid design. Those in the landscape profession need to become stronger designers, smarter conceptualists and better architects of the land. Solid design endures. We have to embrace the idea of invention to provide more sensitive and responsive alternatives, to challenge the emerging 'green design' convention. The idea of engineering cannot be allowed to dominate the expression of a place in terms of its design.

Michael Van Valkenburgh

In any field, the most fertile territory for creativity is often found at its margins, where it intersects with other fields. As we strive to activate the full potential of the landscape medium, I think the best place to begin will be at its junctures with science, art and urbanism. For instance, we all recognize that it is urgent that the science of sustainability be better understood in practice, more fully integrated into our work, and more rigorously evaluated for actual performance after a project's completion. Measurable standards might be a useful starting point for this work, but design creativity will depend on understanding the parameters and variables that influence sustainable performance. Landscape practices that could be improved through better scientific engagement include the use of manufactured soil, ecological restorations in urban environments, and growing trees and plants on top of structured platforms (the roofs of parking garages, typically).

Another margin of particular interest to me is art. As the boundary of artistic expression expands, I see a concurrent and deeper consideration of the aesthetic potential of landscape – but on its own artistic terms, not those of architecture or even sculpture, which have both misguided the 'creative' work of some landscape architects in the last century. The idea of 'art' should never be invoked as an excuse for capriciously 'self-expressive' landscape design. There are also tremendous opportunities in the overlap between landscape architecture and urban design. The good news is that we have already moved away from a 20th-century urban-planning practice, in which landscape architects were asked to simply fill in the green areas of a plan. Now they are being brought into the planning process earlier, and are being given more opportunities to positively influence the design of cities. To make a lasting change in the practice of urban design, however, the advantages of landscape methodologies have to be evident in the built work and in the quality of people's lives, not simply in the realm of conference papers and academia. This reinforces the need for more scientific rigour, so that landscape designers are working with solid information that will allow us to know the real social and ecological value of what we build.

As bigger, more complex cities are built around the globe, and as we work to restore and reprogramme abandoned industrial sites, it will be the quality of the landscape that makes the 21st-century metropolis a livable and joyful place for the populace. As well as better engaging the periphery of the field, therefore, one of the great opportunities for landscape designers will be to recognize the avant-garde potential in the most basic and 'old-fashioned' objectives of our discipline.

Louisa Jones

Many gardeners, both professional and amateur, assume their design choices are limited only by budget or personal taste. Slogans that encourage more connected vision, such as 'Think global, act local' and 'Work with, not against nature', have become mere clichés. What might they mean if we were to move beyond the realm of tired polarities: design versus plants; formal versus naturalistic; conceptual versus ecological; even culture versus nature? Why, for example, separate ornamental and useful gardening? Any one feature, any one plant, can look good, but can also provide food and drink, scent, health and household aids, homemade pest controls, home crafts. This kind of multiple gardening – multi-function, multi-pleasure – has been practised for millennia as the vernacular (a term better known among architects). To paraphrase one definition of vernacular design, it is made of predominantly local materials, reveals a high regard for craftsmanship and quality, is ecologically apt, fits in well with local-climate flora, fauna and way of life, is human in scale, and embodies a sensual frugality that results in true elegance. A major aim of vernacular design is climate control throughout the year – planning and planting as much for floods as for droughts, regulating temperature, providing sources of energy in the form of firewood, wind or solar power. Creativity is the essence of vernacular gardening where necessity has always been the mother of invention. Home-style 'land art' appeals to gardeners of all ages. Why not bring back the energy-saving clothes line as an example of ephemeral domestic art?

The Mediterranean version is a particularly good model because, like the cuisine of the region, it offers infinite regional and personal variation yet is adaptable worldwide. It is locally based and economical, but capable of great refinement; pleasure-giving, healthy and accessible to all. It also lends itself to intelligent eco-tourism, playing a growing role in evolving rural economies. But there is another, deeper reason. The human footprint has been heavier in the Mediterranean than almost anywhere else in the world, and yet, as recent studies affirm, 'there is often more biodiversity in a single square kilometre in the Mediterranean than in any area a hundred times larger in the northern parts of Europe'. Scientists attribute this wealth in part to 'co-evolution' between mankind and other species – not everywhere and not all the time, especially today, but recurrent and persistent.

One historian noted: 'The view that humans have had almost entirely negative impacts on nature – widespread among environmental historians, historical geographers, ecologists and environmentalists – paradoxically perpetuates the old Western stereotypes of humanity as active, dominating and separate from a nature that is passive and static. A view more in tune with late 20th-century empirical data and current ecological theory would emphasize that relationships between humans and nature are interactive and embedded within a kaleidoscopic environment in which little or nothing is permanent.'

Multiple gardening the Mediterranean way is both very old and very new.

PROAP

LISBON, PORTUGAL

Urban design that blends strident Modernism with
a romantic environmental and agricultural sensibility.

João Nunes and Carlos Ribas are the landscape architects who lead Proap, a partner-ship founded in 1989 that now has some thirty employees, including twelve landscape architects and one architect. Most of their work is in Portugal, though the firm increas-ingly secures commissions in Spain and Italy, with other projects in Angola and Algeria. A step-change in the development of the company occurred in the mid-1990s, when it was awarded the commission for the Expo 98 park in Lisbon.

Proap has developed an extremely complex and detailed methodology and phi-losophy, which it struggles to elucidate (in the English language, at least). There is an emphasis on 'decoding' space and place, which is achieved via linguistic theory. 'The landscape is a text,' Nunes says, 'an assembly of signs that translates the sense of the actions that produced it'. Of decoding, Nunes states: 'In Proap's characteristic meth-odological procedures, decodification means full understanding of the mechanisms that are present in the landscape, the acting and determinant metabolisms of the rela-tionships between actors, meaning understanding a given landscape far beyond image.' This indicates that the firm tries to find out everything that is particular about a site. Nunes concludes: 'Proap's position is precisely the position of not having a common strategy besides the attempt at decoding. Each model is a model, as good as the next, and we intend to act within its own rules – you just have to understand it.'

Certain tangible preoccupations emerge out of the generalizing theoretical morass, including an abiding interest in the movement of the sun and concomitant shade, and the notion of the limits or boundaries of landscape spaces. As for the work, it speaks for itself.

03

04

05

06

01-06 The São Lourenço Garden consists of two
contrasting areas: a swimming-pool terrace
with an undulating sunbathing area on the
first floor, and a geometric garden of raised
beds on the ground floor.

09

10

07-10 The elegant new approach to Silves Castle includes decked walkways that follow the contours of the existing terraces. A new entrance facility is located halfway up the route to the castle.

The São Lourenço Garden (2009), in Lisbon, covers the ground-level patio and first-floor roof terraces of a new residential development. As the project developed, Proap was also commissioned to redesign significant aspects of the surrounding public realm. 'The aim of the composition', the company states, 'was the creation of legible, clear and harmoniously arranged human-scaled spaces.' At ground level, the central space is defined by slate paving, which establishes a material link with the surrounding buildings, while the garden area is composed of raised planters and a water feature – a geometric pool filled with a grid of paving slabs – whose focal point is a polished concrete wall endowed with light and water. The second floor is split into two distinct parts: the southern section has a space for sunbathing and two swimming pools, while the northern end has a recreational garden that is punctuated by playground elements.

At Silves Castle (2008) in the Algarve region, also in Portugal, Proap was asked to redefine access to the 11th-century castle from the town below, with new walkways and entrance facilities. There are three main routes – two for pedestrians, one for restricted traffic – to the new entrance building. From here, using the existing terraces below the building, Proap introduced a system of paths in wooden decking and fine gravel that allows a gradual approach up to the castle, while at the same time offering fine views over the city and surrounding countryside.

In 2009, Proap won first prize in an international competition to redevelop the riverfront at Antwerp, in the Netherlands, which incorporates various structures along a tidal defence barrier that protects the city. The firm's masterplan envisaged certain areas that are more liable to flooding – or regular tidal fluctuations – as temporary landscape spaces – a dynamic landscape, therefore, that will change according to tide patterns. The suitability of different landscape systems for different parts of the riverfront is identified through the use of a 'planning game' (*kaaiplan-spel*), which contains typological pieces of the toolkit.

11–14 Proap's competition-winning design for the riverfront at Antwerp included a flood-defence system that can also be used for a variety of civic activities. What is novel about the scheme is the way the company incorporated the prospect of intermittent flooding in space, which could be used for other specific purposes when not affected by water levels.

RADERSCHALL PARTNER

MEILEN, SWITZERLAND

Classic functional design, but realized on a human scale
and with human emotions in mind.

Led by Sybille Aubort Raderschall, Markus Fierz and Roland Raderschall, this firm
was founded in 1990 and now has ten employees. The company describes their methodology as 'research-based', with work encompassing housing estates, schools, hospitals, city streets and plazas, office, commercial and industrial spaces, and home gardens
and parks, mainly in Switzerland.

At the MFO Park (2002) in north Zürich – a postindustrial site that was formerly
the MFO machine works – the firm introduced bold new avenues of trees and accentuated the presence of the Binzmühle brook, which itself is lined with birch trees. Their
main intervention, however, was the 'park house', a vine-covered, multi-storey steel
building, designed in collaboration with architects Burckhardt & Partners. This large,
U-shaped framework partially encloses a huge, rectangular space, with visitors able to
experience it at different levels. There are benches and pools at ground level, where the
cables for vines (wisteria, grapevine, ampelopsis and parthenocissus) can be seen at
their starting points, as well as yew, birch hedges and flowering shrubs such as honeysuckle, *Actinidia arguta*, *Clematis maximowicziana* and *Aristolochia durior*.

Raderschall suggests that this intervention is a reference to the massive industrial
buildings that characterize this part of Zürich. The company calls the structure 'an
old-fashioned trellis, open on three sides and veiled in lush plant growth', with four
'chalices' of foliage surrounding a circular reflecting pool. The space between the
double walls of the framework is shot through with flights of stairs, colonnades and
projecting loggias. At the very top, on the roof, is the sun deck, surrounded by filigreed
foliage. Rainwater is collected and redistributed via an irrigation system; the plants at

01 At the MFO Park in Zürich, a huge metal framework delineates the indoor-outdoor building. Vines climb up wires inside the structure and also clad the exterior, creating a park that is transformed with each season.

02-03 This courtyard at the Innenhof Westpark is filled with grey-basalt gravel and fringed with mass plantings of hydrangeas. Wisteria clambers up wires that are suspended from another wire, slung across the length of the courtyard.

higher levels are sited in irrigated troughs. The firm sums up the sensual appeal of the place: 'The park undergoes pronounced seasonal change. In winter, the construction comes to light, only to vanish again under a layer of green during the growing period. In the autumn, the park gleams with the red of wild vine. The play of light and shade plunges the interior spaces into a series of ever-changing moods. The summer's heat is pleasantly tempered. At night, the structures of the square and atrium are lit up from within and seem to take on three-dimensional form. A space saturated with the patter of rain, dancing shadows on the gravel ground, the twitter of birds in the leafy walkways, a bustle in the trompe-l'oeil architecture, a stroll up and down aromatic green stairways, a summer's night in an "opera" loge.'

At the Innenhof Westpark (2002), an office building also in Zürich, Raderschall again utilized the aesthetic of taut, vine-covered wires (in this case, blue wisteria), this time in an open courtyard that the team filled with grey-basalt gravel and lined with hydrangeas, the flowers of which are not cut, but allowed to fade into wintertime.

03

Here, the wires reach up to another, horizontal wire that is slung across the courtyard, creating a harp-like effect and the desired shimmering green space. At the base of the vine, planters are filled with woodland plants such as geraniums and bluebells, along with *Anemone blanda* and *Lonicera japonica*. Three bubbling, black-basalt fountains create a tranquil soundscape.

Raderschall also designs private gardens, such as the Hünerwadel residence (2007) at Küsnacht, above Lake Zürich. The garden at this hillside property was reorganized into three distinct areas: an extension of the living space with a grid of square, steel-framed planting beds that alternate with grasses and Japanese maple trees; a minimalist swimming-pool garden; and a natural-looking upper terrace with mature plane trees and a pond. Maples were also planted on the slope above the house for their dramatic autumn colour. The result is a Modernist architectural garden design with a woodland planting aesthetic.

04-07 The garden at the Hünerwadel residence is ranged across a steep hillside, and features a swimming-pool garden and an 'outdoor room' adjacent to the house.

SANT EN CO

THE HAGUE, NETHERLANDS

Dutch functional Modernism with an austere edge, undercut by
a surprising use of materials and striking sculptural interventions.

Founded in 1990 by Monique de Wette and Edwin Santhagens, who currently employ
seven other young landscape architects, Sant en Co melds a certain Modernist auster-
ity with a delightfully unpredictable exuberance. As they say: 'Standard solutions do
not exist. Starting with a pragmatic conceptual rationale, we design plans, but design
is more than problem-solving. We are also concerned with creating innovative, original plans of beauty, style and artistic expression.' Creative collaboration with clients is
also something this firm actively relishes. They continue: 'A good plan has many
"fathers". The best plans are created by an "intellectual tango" with the client: an interactive and open planning process.'

One of the company's most exciting and challenging recent projects was the revi-
talization of the Roombeek area of the city of Enschede, at the eastern border of the
Netherlands. In 2000, a fireworks factory in this district caught fire and exploded,
razing buildings to the ground and resulting in the deaths of twenty-three people; in
the Netherlands, it is known as the *Vuurwerkramp* (fireworks disaster). Roombeek has
now been rebuilt, and Sant en Co were responsible for the landscape design, working
closely with the local community. The existing street plan was retained as new neighbourhoods were reconfigured, centred on an intersection known as the 'knot'. The
main shopping street, the Roomweg, was redefined by the incorporation into the
landscape scene of the brook that gives the district its name, but which formerly ran
underground, hidden from view. The designers brought the brook up to street level,
allowing it to meander through wide pavement areas, designed to catch the sun.
Informal groupings of trees (*Rhus typhina*), plantings of ferns and strips of grass help

01 The renaissance of the Roombeek district of
   Enschede incorporates a variety of landscape
   typologies, including this running track outside
   school gates in a densely populated residential area.

04

02-03 The Museumlaan is a linear park adjacent
       to a new museum, lined by new private
       residences. One end of the space is now a
       contemporary garden, consisting of strips
       of ornamental grasses.
   04 The brook that gives this district its name
       previously ran underground and has been
       brought to the surface by Sant en Co,
       who also introduced the fragmented
       stepping stones.

create an informal atmosphere conducive to strolling. The shallow brook is filled with a striking array of stepping stones; the fragmented pattern is intended to refer to the 'randomness of nature', the designers say. The waterflow is regulated, so that the brook runs all the time and the sound of water accompanies passers-by.

Another important aspect of the scheme is the Museumlaan, a pedestrian zone related to a new museum. The linear design is defined by four avenues of paulownia trees, interspersed with strips of mown grass and bluebell plantings; contemporary sculpture will also be placed here. A series of private villas built in Modernist style flanks this space, with the limits of the properties demarcated by a long, uniform box-wood hedge that runs the length of the space. One section of the Museumlaan has been turned into a 'contemporary garden', featuring single-species strip-plantings of ornamental grasses. The adjacent *Voorzieningencluster* (facilities cluster) is a mixture of schools, homes, health and care institutions, sports facilities, shops and a theatre, all in a compact urban setting. The philosophy informing the public space is that of multi-functionality; a schoolyard, neighbourhood square and playground all share the same space, while a system of footpaths links these disparate spaces on a human scale, with children especially in mind. One public area adjacent to the school has been set out as a running track, which is car-free during school hours.

THE SHEFFIELD SCHOOL

SHEFFIELD, ENGLAND

At the cutting edge of planting design worldwide, this 'school' takes naturalism to its logical conclusion, often with beguiling effects.

The city of Sheffield in northern England has emerged as the world leader in naturalistic planting, courtesy of two ecological/horticultural researchers at the city's university – James Hitchmough and Nigel Dunnett – who have been pushing the naturalistic creed as far as it can go, beyond what has been achieved by the New Perennials movement (see Piet Oudolf; p. 206). Hitchmough and Dunnett and their colleagues, who together form the Sheffield School, recreate 'plant communities' in public spaces – a largely undesigned aesthetic. The designers do not use planting plans or envisage colour-themed borders, but instead sow seed-mixes inspired by specific native or non-native plant communities, and then allow nature to do the rest, only intervening if one plant seems to be taking over. The aim is to create gardens that look as if they have arisen without human intervention; 'enhanced nature' is what they call it.

Hitchmough and Dunnett say that their urban meadows have been particularly well received and cared for in deprived areas, where bleak sections of common land have been transformed by their plantings. They are passionately committed to the idea that naturalistic plant communities are good not just for the environment, but for our wellbeing, too. Until now, the work of the Sheffield School has mainly been in parks and town centres, since they rely on public funding for their research. Large-scale examples of their work can be found in Newcastle, Telford, Bristol and, of course, Sheffield. In 2012, the most high-profile example of their work will be unveiled in London, where they have been commissioned to create the plantings for the Olympic Park. But increasingly they are acting independently as consultants or landscape designers for enlightened private clients.

01 Moroccan toadflax (*Linaria maroccana*) is prominent in the foreground of a direct-sown annual pictorial meadow by Nigel Dunnett.

02 Detail can be an important factor in pictorial-meadow planting. Here, orange Star of the Veldt hybrids mingle with white *Gypsophila elegans* and cornflower hybrids.

03 Dunnett's annual meadows contain native and non-native species to enhance the aesthetic effect. This mix of sown annuals includes red flax (*Linum grandiflorum* 'Rubrum'), and hybrids of Californian poppy (*Eschscholzia californica*) and corn marigold (*Chrysanthemum segetum*).

04 The North American glade in the Woodland Garden at Sheffield Botanical Gardens, created by Dunnett from a seed mix containing purple coneflower (*Echinacea purpurea*), sown among asters and rudbeckias planted at very low density (one plant per square metre, or 11 sq ft).

05 A pictorial meadow in a residential neighbourhood of Sheffield.

06 Sown Californian poppies create an informal public park on common land, also in Sheffield. The designers claim that colourful meadows in public places encourage outdoor play.

07 *Echinacea pallida* and *Aster macrophyllus* in a sown meadow.

08 A pictorial meadow in another local park in the city, with Shirley poppies (hybrids of *Papaver rhoeas*) in the foreground.

'People have wanted to create the appearance of nature since medieval times,' says Hitchmough. 'The trouble is, they didn't know how to do it.' Hitchmough posits himself and his colleagues as at the cutting edge of a garden movement that grew out of experiments in Germany and Holland in the post-war years. But only now, he believes, do ecologists know enough about plants in the wild to be able to emulate their habitats successfully. Hitchmough's speciality is planting meadows and prairies in open, sunny situations; his work can be seen at the Royal Horticultural Society's show garden at Wisley, in Surrey, and at RHS Harlow Carr in Yorkshire, where he created a moist meadow filled with candelabra primulas. Hitchmough also collaborates regularly with Tom Stuart-Smith (see p. 282) on private commissions, including a garden at Heveningham Hall, in Suffolk, where he has been developing a North American prairie landscape since 2004.

Hitchmough's colleague Nigel Dunnett worked as a garden designer until he was thirty, and thus brings his own particular aesthetic to the mix. 'Where I think I depart from James is that I very much believe in active colour-theming. In terms of planting, it is as designed as any other style,' he states. 'It's just that, rather than producing a planting plan, in which you locate the position of every plant, the design goes into the overall planting mix, giving it spontaneity and dynamism.' Dunnett's main area of interest is in the planting in urban environments of colourful swathes of annual flowers, or 'pictorial meadows'. He talks of the plants mingling and their colours combining as they might in an Impressionist painting, and declares that he can create a meadow with everything he needs – handfuls of seeds – stuffed in his pockets.

'There is a definite strand within the "new naturalism" approach to planting that rejects Jekyllian or painterly notions of colour theory or plant association,' Dunnett says. 'I see myself as mixing in aspects of that more traditional painterly approach, making decisions relating to colour theory and visual appearance as the primary design factors and starting points. Geographical origin, or an attempt to recreate the character of specific semi-natural plant communities from around the world is not as important for me.' Dunnett is also acknowledged as a world authority on green-roof technology, and recently has been devising 'rain gardens' that reuse rainwater.

The key publication related to Hitchmough and Dunnett's work is *The Dynamic Landscape* (2004), in which they stress the social dimension of their proposals and the realities of maintenance levels in the public sector. 'Ecological processes include factors such as regeneration, competition, death and decay, and nutrient recycling,' they write. 'In traditionally cultivated vegetation, irrespective of origin, spatial arrangement and husbandry, we grossly inhibit these processes. That ecological worth may be

13

14

09 A sown annual meadow with purple tansy
    (*Phæcelia tanacetifolia*) amid housing.
10 The planting techniques of the Sheffield
    School are the result of intensive research.
    Here, an allotment plot contains plants that
    are being screened by Hitchmough for their
    suitability for wider landscape use.
11 Sown annual meadow mix by Dunnett in
    the London 2012 Olympic Park, with prairie
    tickseed (*Coreopsis tinctoria*), corn marigold
    hybrids (*Chrysanthemum segetum*), Star
    of the Veldt (*Dimorphotheca sinuata*) and
    cornflower (*Centaurea cyanus*).
12 The designers say that their pictorial
    meadows 'embody the exact opposite of
    a keep-off-the-grass, don't-touch-the-
    flowers mentality'.
13 A green-roof sowing in Sheffield by Dunnett,
    which contains a diverse range of plants.
14 A sown meadow on an urban rooftop, also in
    Sheffield. According to Dunnett, it provides
    a larger area of planting than would often
    be possible on the ground in the same part
    of the city, and is of great value to wildlife.

more tied up in notions of process, rather than a product, is an unsettling idea, as it undermines the foundations of many of our values, which are grounded in commodities, a perspective in time and the current boundaries of the nation state.'

Also operating at the more artistic end of the spectrum is Noël Kingsbury, a plantsman who has been strongly identified with the New Perennials movement in planting design over the past decade or so. 'I'm sceptical about the whole idea of designing with plants,' Kingsbury says, somewhat heretically. 'You can do that up to a point, but then natural processes take over. My aim is a for a much denser, more diverse vegetation than you would normally find in a garden. Weeds can be kept down because the plants self-seed and spread.' Kingsbury has recently completed a number of plantings in this style in the centre of Bristol, and generally undertakes one major private commission each year.

'The key idea is repetition,' Kingsbury continues. 'You can create a rhythm using a few link plants. In a sunny habitat, grasses work best for that, if you just choose one or two. In shade, ferns are good because they have a certain height, and psychologically we expect to see them in woodlands. In moist areas I like to use miscanthus grasses, because although they are not truly wetland plants, they look like stylized reeds and do well. And in dry areas I would go for a Mediterranean maquis look, with those wonderful, rounded santolina and lavender-type plants, all silver and green, with such an evocative scent.' Kingsbury is refreshingly honest about the fact that these 'naturalistic' landscapes are as designed and artificial as any Modernist confection.

15 A roof terrace in Sheffield, planted by
Dunnett. About fifty different plant species
create a 'dry meadow' effect (the roof
receives no irrigation), with a long flowering
season. The planting was set out without a
planting plan, producing a highly naturalistic
aesthetic. Species include sea campion
(*Silene maritima*), sea thrift (*Armeria
maritima*) and *Sisyrinchium striatum*, with
patches of Kniphofia 'Border Ballet' behind.

STEPHEN STIMSON

FALMOUTH / CAMBRIDGE, MASSACHUSETTS, USA

Less truly is more in the case of this minimalist designer, who relies more on natural effects and materials than hardscape.

The goal of this practice, founded in 1992 by Stephen Stimson with four colleagues, is 'to create enduring, innovative landscapes that express cultural values and an environmental ethic'. Their work is 'strongly influenced by minimalism and a modern aesthetic', with a 'focus on clear spatial ordering and efficient site relationships'. It is perhaps the minimalist element of this statement that comes to the fore in the context of landscape design; this is a company that truly dares to do less to create more.

At a garden for a family home in Greenwich, Connecticut (2005), the aim was to build upon a modern sensibility that was respectful of the regional setting. A system of fieldstone walls organizes the 1.6-hectare (4-acre) site into terraces from north to south, creating gentle transitions over the 4.3m (14 ft) drop in elevation along its length. A bronze and mahogany gate, designed by landscape architect Dan Kiley, provides entry onto a gently curving drive, while a rectangular pool quietly sends water over a small weir into a 25m- (82 ft-) long runnel. A row of red maples and holly hedge frame the path to the front door; walkways and steps of monolithic bluestone define site lines and lead into the landscape. The entry walk continues into a birch grove, whose canopy shades the house and forms a foreground for viewing the gardens beyond. Trees were planted at different sizes and the spacing was varied to mimic a woodland's pattern of growth. The ground plane is a continuous band of lily turf, with stripes of bluebells and cinnamon fern for seasonal colour. Terminating the walk on the west side is the pool terrace, framed by stone walls. Dense plantings of Norway spruce, hollies, redbud, rhododendron and witch-hazel screen the busy road; stripes of summer-blooming perennials, including lady's mantle, iris, day lily, fountain grass

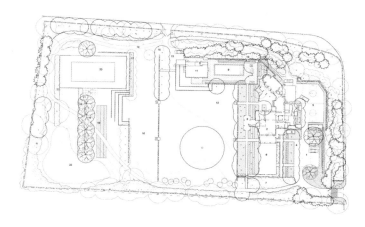

01-06 At this garden for a private residence in
Greenwich, Connecticut, parallel stone
walls organize the site into terraces
that run north to south. A birch grove
shades a dry-laid bluestone walk that
runs in an east-west axis along the
length of the house.

and Russian sage, border the sunny sides of the terrace. Along the terrace's north side, astilbe, ferns and lily turf thrive in the grove's shade. A few steps lead down to a lawn that has been carefully graded to preserve a magnificent elm tree, and further steps continue down to a putting green, and then to a tennis court and shed at a lower level. Yellow-wood, shad, red maple, deciduous holly and blueberries are planted in rows parallel to the terrace walls, while bands of perennials and grasses, including indigo, iris, aster, goldenrod and switch grass, create a linear rhythm.

At a residential project in Chilmark (2007), on Martha's Vineyard, Massachusetts, existing glacial boulders and mature trees have been woven into a design of minimal walls and terraces to 'ground' the house on its site. Grading and sight lines are amplified by stone walls that underscore the dramatic contours of the local terrain. Manmade features of the site remain respectful of the native landscape in that they have been inserted into the spaces created by larger existing trees and boulders. The clients use the site as a vacation retreat, with a programme consisting of a main house, guest house, basketball court, parking court and swimming pool. As collectors of modern art and photography, they wanted a design that was minimal, understated and connected to the site. Stimson approached the project with the image of a minimal planting palette that would celebrate the vegetation of the island. Native oak, maple, cedar, witch-hazel, bluestem grasses, rose mallow and ferns create understated garden areas. Throughout the site, the geometry of walls and terraces adjacent to the house and pool contrast with the less ordered landscape of the native meadow and woodland.

The landscape designer and architect worked closely to create a strong continuity between interior and exterior spaces. Concrete pavers lead across the gravel driveway to a wooden boardwalk that passes through the front entry. The boardwalk continues to be read in the wood flooring of the house and rear deck, evolving into a concrete plank walkway that leads towards the pool. This north–south axis functions as a central spine connecting the parking court, entry garden, house and rear lawn. Granite slabs lead informally through the meadow to the pool area, which is built into the hillside to create a dramatic edge between water and distant views.

08

09

10

11

07-11 At this residence on Martha's Vineyard, the minimal planting palette celebrates the indigenous vegetation of the island. Native oak, maple, cedar, witch-hazel, bluestem grasses, rose mallow and ferns create understated garden areas.

TOM STUART-SMITH

LONDON, ENGLAND

Designer who fuses sure spatial awareness with an acute planting sensibility, honed from the British herbaceous tradition.

If any designer epitomizes the state of British garden design at the moment, it is Tom Stuart-Smith. His work is a good gauge of contemporary planting style, as it unites the 'tapestry' effect of intense herbaceous-border design, in the tradition of Gertrude Jekyll and the Arts and Crafts movement, with the influx of ecological planting ideas from Holland and Germany – the so-called 'New Perennials' style, with its swaying drifts of grasses and tall perennials, arrayed in naturalistic fashion. What this means in practice is that Stuart-Smith's designs are lent a clear structure that is formed by just a few species of grasses, typically miscanthus, stipa or carex, and complemented by plantings of powerful plants, which are repeated through the border design and organized with care and panache. The main difference between the British and continental interpretations of the New Perennials is in the former's continued emphasis on colour and as wide a range of plants as possible. A pared-down palette is emphatically not the British way, and this is echoed in Stuart-Smith's work, which unites horticultural complexity with structural planning.

Stuart-Smith began his career as a landscape architect, working on historical conservation projects, before bursting to prominence as a garden designer with a string of six gold-medal winning gardens at Chelsea Flower Show. His landscape training means that he is unafraid to think spatially, even at such an avowedly horticultural event; perhaps his best Chelsea garden utilized Corten steel (a favourite material) as a linking device, offset by the cinnamon-coloured bark of the underestimated shrub *Viburnum rhytidophyllum*. In 2002, Queen Elizabeth II commissioned Stuart-Smith to design a new garden next to the entrance drive at Windsor Castle. Other

03

04

02 The new walled garden at Broughton Grange
is walled on just two sides, to allow for
uninterrupted views of the Oxfordshire
countryside. It is divided into three stepped
terraces, with the lower one serving as
a conceptual and visual linking device
between the garden and the landscape.

03 At a private residence in Hampshire, Stuart-
Smith created a garden of grasses and
perennials for a client with an enthusiasm
for ornate Victorian clipped topiary (and
for chickens, which run free in the garden).

04 The walled garden shown here is one of
three distinct areas at a coastal residence
in Norfolk. Stuart-Smith's signature Corten
steel was used to line the raised beds; he
notes that rusted metal can often be seen
on the beaches in this area, which made it
appropriate as a material.

major projects include the comprehensive redesign and replanting of the Victorian
parterres at Trentham Gardens, in Staffordshire, achieved in collaboration with Piet
Oudolf (see p. 206) and Dominic Cole of Land Use Consultants.

At Broughton Grange (1998), in North Oxfordshire, Stuart-Smith oversaw the
construction of an entirely new walled garden, set at one remove from the house.
Walled on two sides, with ha-has on the other boundaries, the space is divided up into
three identical terraces, each with a different planting regime and soil structure
(Mediterranean in feel at the top; damp foliage plants in the middle). The central terrace contains a long, rectangular pool with stepping stones, and looks down onto an
abstract parterre of box hedges, laid out in a pattern derived from a microscopically
detailed photograph of leaves from the surrounding birch, oak and ash trees. Clipped
yew domes mark the track of a public path (almost inviolable in British law), and act
as symbolic 'walkers' themselves, as the path is barely used. The garden was all about
the tension between the walled garden as a 'container', Stuart-Smith says, and its relationship to the landscape, which is invited in by means of the lack of walls.

Stuart-Smith undertakes a large number of commissions for private clients, and
something of his range is shown in these pages. In an urban environment, he recently
completed a terraced garden in North London (2008) that relies solely on clipped box,
tree ferns and hakenochloa grass, with climbers planted against one wall.

05

06

05-06 Tree ferns and box balls define this small North London garden, designed to be viewed all year round from the windows at the rear of the house. Passers-by can peep over the wall from the pavement to see the extravaganza within.

07 The courtyard garden at the Connaught Hotel in London is designed to be viewed from this angle only. Clipped box and a cloud-pruned *Ilex crenata* are balanced with the swirling rill, while a projection of the moon on the far wall is reflected in the water, creating a shimmering effect.

07

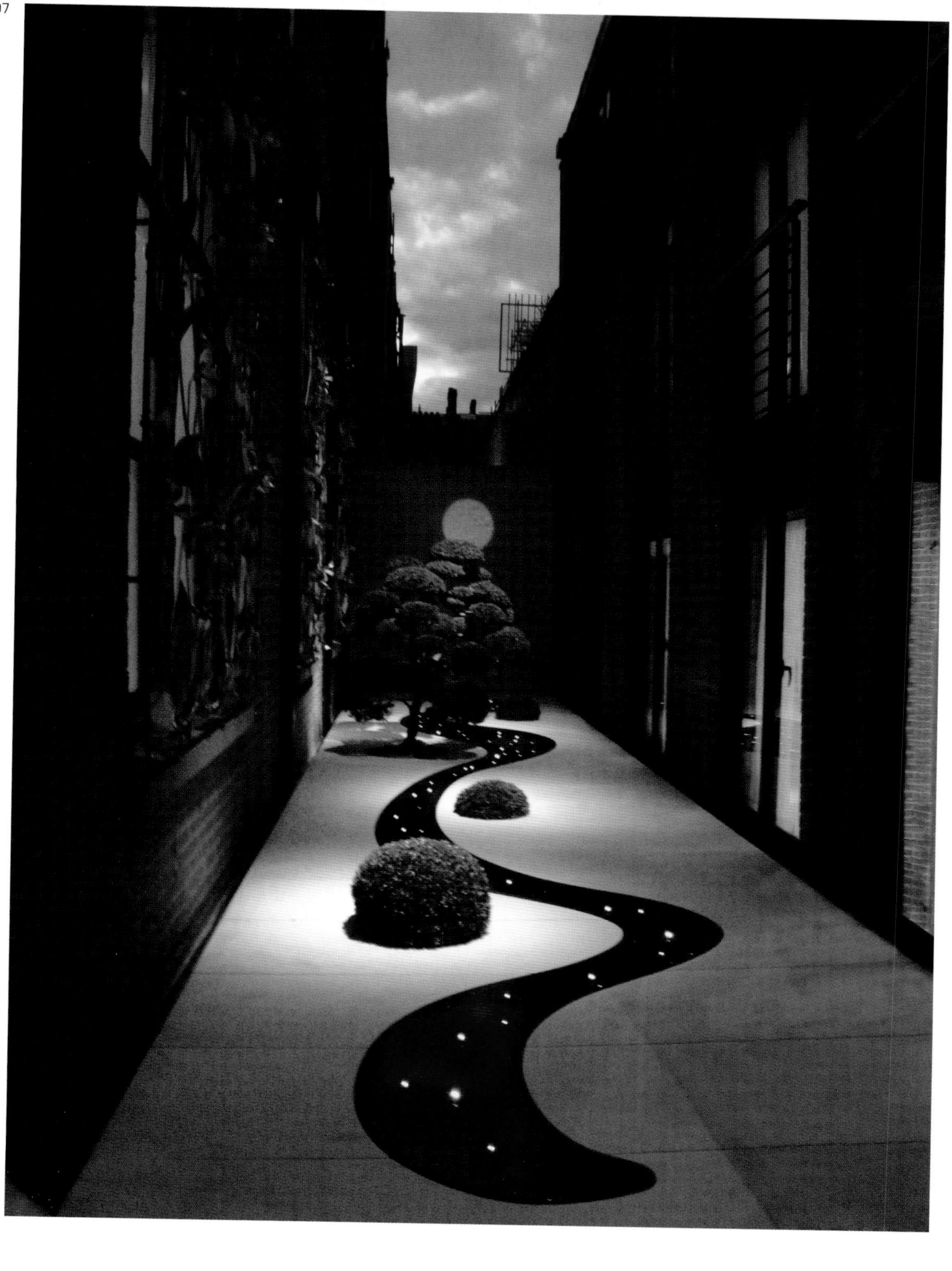

SURFACE DESIGN

SAN FRANCISCO, CALIFORNIA, USA

Working at all scales, this company offers the epitome
of glamorous outdoor living on the domestic scale.

Surface Design was established in 2001 under the leadership of James A. Lord, Roderick Wyllie and Geoff di Girolamo. The stated aims of the company are conventional enough: 'We create projects that have a strong relationship to people and the natural environment. We are passionate about craftsmanship and sustainability'. This is difficult to achieve in practice, of course, as this firm succeeds in doing, across a wide range of scales, from public parks and municipal streetscapes to private estates.

One of the firm's most successful commissions was for the Peterson residence (2010), in Tiburon, California. This sculptural project reflects the unique agenda of the clients, who, the designers say, are passionate art collectors and thoughtful parents, committed to the idea of the landscape being experienced and enjoyed by their children. Surface Design envisaged a landscape that incorporated several distinct spaces woven through the architecture, while also capturing the views and topography. The entrance to the site is punctuated by a folding ipe deck, projecting from the interior of the residence. Here, the planting includes numerous foliage plants, such as Japanese cut-leaf maples, bamboos and ferns. The lawn offers views of San Francisco Bay and the rolling landscape to the north, playfully abstracting the hills beyond visually, while creating a series of distinct play spaces, including a 'hobbit house' and a 'rabbit-hole hill'. Sculptural pieces from the clients' collection are dotted around the garden.

The Museo del Acero Horno[3] (2007), in Monterrey, Mexico, was a collaborative venture aimed at transforming a decommissioned blast furnace and brownfield site into a museum dedicated to the region's rich legacy of steel production. In 1986 the city reclaimed the former steel works, and eleven years later the 70m- (230 ft-) high

03

04

01 The view from the Peterson residence in Tiburon, California, is prefaced by the artificial landscape of grass hillocks, introduced in reference to the landscape beyond. The mounds contain hiding places for the clients' children.

02-04 The rest of the garden's design represents a careful balance between hard landscaping in the form of stone and gravel paths, an ipe deck that leads to the front door, and an informal woodland planting chosen for foliage appeal.

furnace emerged as a new focal point for the modern park. Steel, much of it reclaimed from the site, was used extensively to help define plazas and terraces. Ore-embedded rails were also used for the outdoor exhibit spaces, and machinery unearthed during excavation was incorporated into the design. Two water features were integral to the design narrative. In the main esplanade, the steel plates that formerly clad the exterior of the main hall were used to make a stepped canal, over which water cascades. The 200m- (656 ft-) long canal alludes to the tracks used daily to bring in the thousands of tons of raw materials. At the entrance, it culminates in a fountain, a grid of rocks visibly embedded with ore. This trompe-l'oeil effect evokes the caustic heating process once used to extract ore, but instead of steam, it generates a cooling mist that blows over the plaza. All of the storm water run-off is treated in a series of on-site runnels,

and a green-roof system was introduced on all the buildings. One of the most striking roofs is planted with drought-tolerant sedums, contained by what appears to be a floating steel disk. A circular viewing deck allows visitors to take in the surrounding landscape, including the distant Sierra Madres, which are echoed in the roof's mounded shape. The landscape below was planted with native grasses and rushes (*Eragrostis intermedia*, *Juncus effusus* and *Baumea rubiginosa*) and trees: cedar elm (*Ulmus crassifolia*) and blue paloverde (*Parkinsonia florida*).

San Francisco's characteristic steep slopes presented a problem at the Rieders residence (2009), which the firm addressed by reformulating the garden spaces into a three-tiered experience. Beginning at the lowest level, visitors exit the parking garage and prepare to climb steps up to the house. Here, a fountain and pool in wood-textured concrete slabs were introduced as a calming note. The material changes to cedar as one climbs to the main level, where an existing oak tree was retained and the plantings were chosen to reflect Northern California's plant palette. Native grasses and other drought-tolerant plants form a backdrop of muted greens and dusky plums that harmonize against the stained black cedar decking. Finally, the visitor climbs another flight to a viewing platform with expansive views across the bay towards the Golden Gate Bridge. The quiet lower 'grotto' is composed of geometric paving, metal planters and lush, shade-loving plants, including *Woodwardia radicans*, *Helleborus orientalis* and Persicaria 'Red Dragon'. The sunny hillside is covered with a crimson sea of *Tradescantia pallida*, accented with a mix of agaves, aeoniums and sedums, while the board-formed walls are softened with wispy plumes of *Pennisetum alopecuroides*. A path of square pavers leading to the top deck appears to float above a soft bed of fescue naïve, bordered by a mix of *Muhlenbergia rigens* and *Anigozanthos flavidus*.

05-07 The Museo del Acero Horno³, in Monterrey, Mexico, is dominated by the blast furnace. Reusing fragments of steel found on site, Surface Design introduced green roofs and other large-scale decorative features to complement the massive scale of the former steel works without competing with it.

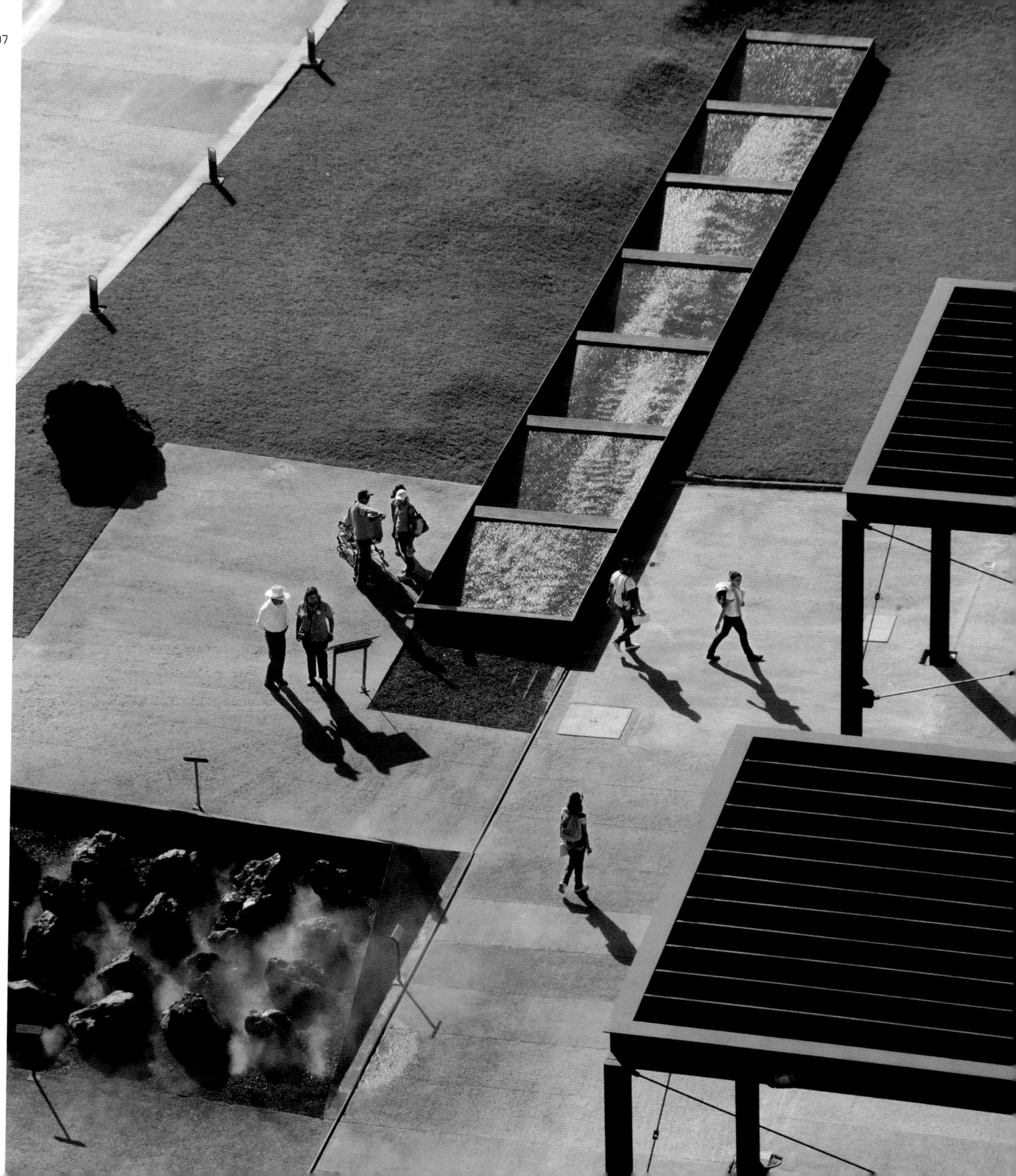

08-11 At the Rieders residence in San Francisco,
a three-tiered garden was created from an
awkward and little-used space, beginning
with a concrete 'grotto' and fountain pool at
parking-garage level, and rising to two more
levels, culminating in a viewing platform.

09

10

11

THE FUTURE OF
LANDSCAPE DESIGN:
FORUM TWO

A selection of the world's most influential landscape and
garden designers and critics were asked to respond briefly
to the following simple question: 'What are the greatest
opportunities and challenges facing landscape designers
in the early 21st century?'

Ron Lutsko

Through technology we have an unprecedented ability to alter our environment. Simultaneously, habitat, in the form of continuous corridors, must permeate people's environs as a likely prerequisite to the survival of humanity as we know it. The notion that people, acting as individual stewards, can perpetuate a sustainable culture-wide relationship with the natural world is obsolete. No longer hunters, gatherers or, for the most part, farmers, our relationship with ecological systems is now dependent on an infrastructure controlled by amorphous entities. This has resulted in a population unaware of, unable to comprehend and profoundly alienated from the rest of the natural world. It therefore follows that landscape architects, although attempting to beautify the environment, generally create landscapes that emerge as unrelated to and isolated from the ecological processes that sustain us. These landscapes typically remove habitat and create ecological vacuums while concealing the infrastructure that brings them life support. This creates a barrier to any dialogue or understanding between people living in these built landscapes and ecological systems.

We must contribute to a new paradigm. I believe this cannot occur until we move beyond the current attitude where people and nature are thought of as separate entities, where our role is to preserve nature as an 'other' entity. We must move to a paradigm that redefines our relationship with the natural world; one that recognizes that people are an integrated piece of the Earth's ecological system and places people as part of nature, and understands and emphasizes the role of people as participants in a greater planetary ecology.

Landscape architects can have a pivotal role in shifting our position on these issues. To realize this, landscapes must be created that connect people with the greater ecology, thus enriching and enlightening human experience. I am not suggesting, however, that we indulge in restoration, or in the practice of recreating the natural landscape; this should be left to the restoration ecologists (albeit integrated with our role). Future landscapes must thoughtfully incorporate a number of topics. Through design they must incorporate ecological systems, recognizing this as the basis of our physical and spiritual survival. They must honestly and eloquently incorporate and express technology and infrastructure, our cultures' true connection to nature, and they must address the significance of the vernacular, acknowledging the powerful meanings it carries in the landscape. They must also function as art, both didactic and passive, to tap the profound potential for experiencing the landscape. As designers of the outside world, we can engage people by presenting information in the context of the highest level of design – we must not ignore the power of beauty and experience. When expressed in the form of thoughtful and sophisticated design, the endemic environment becomes part of daily life, people experience the processes and rhythms of nature, and habitat integrates with and assumes the fabric of the built environment. The resulting examples can suggest a new direction in landscape architecture; one that creates healthy environments, reconciles the relationship between the natural world and centralized technology, and reconnects people with the processes of both.

Lodewijk Baljon

Globalization means that we encounter more of the same, that our environment becomes more general, more common and less genuine. The quest for authenticity is a challenge that must be taken up particularly by landscape architects.

Landscape architecture is about cultivating the place, about transforming the site. By nature it has to deal with the history of the place. But that is only half the story. Heritage is meaningless without contemporary culture, without the present-day production of culture. In our changing environment, we have a need for meaning, mostly expressed through marketing, lifestyles, commercial identities and theme parks. But what we should be looking for is a living, lived and experienced culture. By embedding design in a broader cultural context, landscape architecture can give a sense of place and a sense of time.

In our designs, I am always looking for beautiful contrasts that form a relationship when seen in a larger context. This cohesion is based on the landscape: the history of the place; and the morphology of the ground that lies beneath. The opportunity for landscape architects is to bring this notion of landscape into design at all scales – from gardens to urban developments – and by so doing, to create a sense of authenticity that has emerged from the place itself, as opposed to ideas or themes that have been introduced by a designer.

Ken Smith
'Biglittleskipthemiddle'
Issues of scale are among the fundamental challenges facing landscape architecture as we head into the 21st century. In contemporary practice, we are operating in a world where we are asked with near simultaneity to conceptualize and design large-scale landscapes that range from the restoration of ecological systems, the design of entire

waterfronts, and the development of comprehensive plans for new towns and urban districts, all the way down to the small scale of tiny courtyards or private plots. Tackling these challenges will require expertise in varying levels of thinking and practice.

Much of design practice lacks conceptual clarity at the highest level, while simultaneously lacking attention to the details of craft. It is stuck in the nebulous middle, a fuzzy realm of appropriated products and forms and borrowed ideas. At a fundamental level, good design is the struggle between deductive and inductive processes. We are trained in the rational or deductive 'top-down' process of analysis, alternatives assessment and synthesis of design. In this realm, we work with the systems and organization of landscapes, defining typical conditions and seeking cohesive resolution of order and harmony. But often it is the reverse of this, the 'bottom-up' or inductive methodology that produces the most salient ideas for a design. This is a realm that is more opportunistic, looking for the exceptions to the rule, and the aspects or conditions of a place that are atypical or singular. I find there is something in the unusual particulars of a site, its specific history or context, which becomes the genesis of a design idea tempered with the abstract ideas and ordering devices that come from outside the site. This struggle between deductive and inductive methodology requires both openness to seeing things as they are and a rigour in thinking, and producing strategies of how things could be.

Paolo Pejrone
'Dreams and Hopes'
Every garden, large and small, can be a happy and protected version of nature: a happy garden with happy plants that are well planted and correct for the place. A garden 'going on', not a garden 'against'. A garden where mulching is the most sought-after and important duty, and where no miles are expended in transportation. Garden happiness can be conceived as a regulated and programmed living microcosm of nature, where animals and all natural life can also be happy and healthy. No poisons, no chemical manures, where safe and wise mulching provides a happy and healthy future for the plants.

A modern garden can be a disorderly garden. Precision can be a problem, a worry, a frustration. Nature does not like to be too regimented. A good disorder, a marshalled disorder, can be the real order – a garden where nettles and weeds are also natural guests (perhaps not loved, but quietly accepted). A simple life, where 'work' is simple and basic, where dead leaves are welcome, and where (especially in Italy) the grass on the lawn is allowed to become dry and patchy in summer. Plants should be chosen that are appropriate to the local climate, and not be artificially forced into it. But they do not have to be 'local' themselves: the garden is all about acceptance, hospitality. The garden could be the glory of globalization: a huge, well-articulated melting pot of worldwide botanical riches. A happy new world of gardening that will lead, in turn, to the same for the garden's structure and architecture.

Gavin Keeney

The greatest challenge facing landscape designers and landscape architects in the early 21st century is to resist the so-called machinic tendencies of landscape urbanism – that is, the conversion of landscape to completely artificial and inhuman agency (data, information, infrastructure, etc). This late-modern tendency to instrumentalize everything resists what is most needed in landscape design, in the sense that the 'given' (the already existing beauty and intelligence of natural systems) is slowly being extinguished for totally manmade artifice, none of which is sustainable in the long run, and much of which is pernicious or inhuman.

It is not so much a balance that needs to be struck as a new understanding of what constitutes the conditions of what we call 'landscape', or what comes into designed landscapes from previously existing systems – natural, cultural and otherwise. The misappropriation of Gilles Deleuze's idea of the singular (a self-organized or autopoietic system) has, in turn, brought to landscape architecture an ill-advised determinism that almost always translates into the abdication of creative agency. Landscape needs to be dealt with once again as an art form, as opposed to a pseudo-scientific endeavour.

Kate Cullity

Landscape design is a cultural and social act operating within the nexus between art and science. Our challenge is to awaken the rich potential that resides within this overlap of disciplines through a reinvigoration of the connection between beauty and the environment.

By beauty we mean the all-encompassing somatic and visceral kind, rather than the purely visual. Beauty which has the power to awaken a reimagining of new ways to relate to, care for and be in the environment. Such an experience of beauty provides a conduit between the senses and reason, between what is known and what could be.

The challenge is to find new connections, to create conceptual and experiential hybrids across the seemingly paradoxical lines that regulate our thinking about and experience of the landscape; to not be tied to the dichotomies of cultural and natural, human-made and elemental, formal and informal. Our landscapes can transgress across fields, seeking out overlap and hybridization. They can be wild and urbane, social and ecological, aesthetic and environmentally responsive, visual and performative, challenging and familiar, delightful and serious. They can be beautiful and sustainable.

Penelope Hobhouse

I first started creating gardens and landscapes almost thirty years ago. I had no formal training, but was approached by clients who had read my books about colour and design. Usually, especially in the United States, I worked with an architect who dealt with the more technical side, until I established my own office and worked with a trained associate. I suppose my forte was perfecting a strong, quite formal framework, and then creating a planting jungle inside it, mainly dictated by colour themes.

Today it is not enough to have a 'good eye' and horticultural experience. Design has become much more of a science. Every site has differing demands, and requires an in-depth knowledge of ecological factors and sustainability. This provides opportunity, but also creates new challenges. Any manmade landscape is essentially artificial, an exercise in aesthetics and a defiance of nature. Can we go too far in trying to reconcile the 'natural' look with beauty? There is always a right place in which to imitate nature, but absolutely no need to slavishly copy a lost wilderness.

Mario Terzic

In terms of using their expertise, I see the biggest opportunity for landscape designers to be the re-evaluation of dated or 'dead' areas of landscape, so that they may be converted into 'premium' space for living and leisure purposes. Those 'fallow' spaces, which were previously used for industrial purposes, as roadways or for agriculture, can become parkland; historic gardens might be transformed into democratic spaces, where people can experience the joy of life; sport grounds could be converted into gardens of movement and contemplation.

The challenge is artistic. The jury-crowned 'greening' of pre-ordained competition areas by landscape architects simply will not do! Deriving inspiration only from the contemporary art market won't be enough, either. Plants, water, people, weather, animals, time – these are the topics to be considered when planning radically new concepts of space. Translating these ideas into reality will bring about the most comprehensive artworks of the 21st century.

Marc Treib

'Dark Clouds on the Horizon'

It's difficult to be optimistic about anything these days. Climate change, continual warfare, economic collapse, the threat of terrorism – yes, it's difficult to be optimistic. And I don't think it's much better in the field of landscape architecture. On the one hand, the legal necessity for environmental reviews may have given landscape architects and planners greater clout than at any time since Frederick Law Olmsted secured comprehensive urban planning and park systems late in the 19th century. Citizen participation may diminish the purity (and at times the quality) of many landscape-design schemes, but of course any definition of quality is certainly open to debate.

In a democratic society, decisions can't be centralized and delivered top-down without some form of popular review and response. Maybe that's a good thing. This so-called field of 'landscape urbanism' may be a good thing as well, demonstrating the need to consider every design decision more broadly, to look well beyond the limits of the site, and above or below its surface. But claiming that infrastructure is urbanism is like saying the digestive tract is your body – while supporting the body and necessary for its operation, it is hardly the body in itself. Will following the path of sustainability as the sole criterion lead us back to the social and ecological determinism of the 1960s and '70s? The landscapes that resulted may or may not have achieved those desired ends, but few of them were remarkable in any experiential or aesthetic way. It's difficult to be optimistic these days.

In recent years, the word 'sustainability' has been on just about everyone's lips – including corporate lips – second only, perhaps, to the term 'global warming'. The latter cites the greater problem; the former, a possible means for its solution. But these two terms have been so overused and exploited for profit as well as good that they have achieved a degree of meaninglessness, with LEEDs certification today anointed as the only worthy design criterion. I am troubled by any design addressed to a single goal or parameter (including purely aesthetic acts removed from functional or social purpose).

Might not a better approach be to adopt the adverb 'sustainably' to describe how we should design, rather than posing the noun 'sustainability' as a single goal? Or, to put it a different way, to use an ecological consciousness to guide the way we design for a greater purpose? Quality cannot be quantified.

Sadly, we often stop at the level of the native plant or the green roof, rather than considering their use as vehicles for achieving an aesthetic level beyond the merely operational. The photographer Edward Weston once wrote that one should photograph a thing 'not for what it is, but for what else it is'. Achieving that 'what else' is what makes landscape design an art. Without such aspirations, we operate only at the level of environmental plumbing (which environmental scientists tend to do much better than landscape architects). Plumbers are needed, of course, but so too are artists. Rather than considering the situation as an either/or, I prefer to think of it as a both/ and, with the ultimate goal being to elevate pragmatics to the level of poetics.

Olmsted, the nominal father of American landscape architecture, considered himself an artist, one imbued with a social conscience, environmental awareness and knowledge far beyond his times. I would also suggest that at least some design practice can be, and should be, a form of research – or at the very least, applied research. Admittedly, given the broad field of parameters that constrain even the smallest design project, we can never achieve the focused study possible under laboratory conditions. But that is not to say that even an artwork or small garden does not itself constitute a laboratory of sorts. When Gertrude Jekyll created her celebrated herbaceous borders, she operated as both scientist and artist. To achieve her aesthetic goals – goals that conjoined colour with blooming time and leaf textures with pollen – she required a deep knowledge of plants, soils, fertilizers and climates, as well as colour theory and, one might add, relevant artistic movements. Jekyll's gardening was both scientific experimentation and aesthetic pursuit, yet she is best known as a garden artist. Jekyll also understood what else the plants of the garden could be, and that's why we hold her work in such high regard.

Given our finite resources, I would also suggest simplicity as a means by which to design: a simplicity of form that yields a complexity of experience. Simplicity should not be equated with reduction, per se. In the West we tend to think of simplicity as a state acquired by leaving things out. Instead, could we not think of simplicity as the product of putting things in? But rather than overlaying them, or juxtaposing them as identifiable fragments, suppose we compress a multitude of aspects into simple forms – forms that read as simple, although incorporating worlds in themselves, like the residue of past eras trapped in amber? If we regard simplicity as condensation or distillation, rather than as reduction or elimination, we may achieve places that are less intrusive yet more rewarding, less fashionable yet more enduring. I believe that through condensation we create a landscape architecture that engages people more profoundly, while being more sympathetic to the environment. Simplicity may not always provide the jazzy image so beloved of the student, the young practitioner or the fashion editor, especially when viewed only on a computer screen. But it will be far more substantial in a life rendered not as a virtual reality, but within the reality in which we live.

How might we surpass the merely functional, the merely sustainable, using simplicity as a guide for creating an engaging landscape? The Patio de los Naranjos (courtyard of the oranges), in Seville, provides a beautiful model. Whether to invoke an image of paradise, as some writers have suggested, or simply to provide a refreshing transition to prayer, the makers of the courtyard landscape proposed a grove of orange trees. There was a problem, though. The climate of Seville is basically that of the desert – about 51cm (20 in) of rainfall a year, with almost none falling during the summer months. Orange trees cannot grow under the natural conditions of the site; irrigation was required. In the right hands and minds, however, irrigation became the device by which to structure the garden, ultimately yielding an aesthetic of order and grace. A grid of rills connects the trees, rills that may be closed or opened to allow, divert or stopper the nourishing current. Add to that level overflowing fountains executed in a white marble that contrast noticeably with the rougher red brick of the paving, the uniformly superb detailing and the glint of the oranges in the sunlight, and the result is perfection.

To my mind this is a superbly sustainable landscape. Not because it emulates the natural landscape that once characterized the site, which it does not, but because it understands natural systems and uses them responsibly for greater aesthetic and experiential purpose. The Courtyard of the Oranges is special because its makers sought more from its creation than any merely mimetic landscape design or measurable ecological performance. The makers sought 'what else' their courtyard could be. And I believe they found it. Can we find our own contemporary equivalent to this courtyard landscape before time runs out? The dark clouds on the horizon threaten; it's difficult to be optimistic. But there may be hope.

SWA GROUP

OFFICES IN CALIFORNIA AND TEXAS, USA

International firm with scores of large-scale projects,
several of which can be counted as innovative and influential.

With scores of projects across some sixty countries, SWA (Sasaki Walker Associates) calls itself 'the biggest little design studio in the world'. It was founded in 1972 by Hideo Sasaki (who died in 2000) and Peter Walker, who left to form his own company in 1983. Like Mesa (see p. 162), another large international company, SWA seeks to avoid the impression of corporatism, or a sense of overly branded design, by splitting itself into smaller parts in order to foster creativity and individuality. SWA has six separate studios, in Sausalito, Laguna Beach, San Francisco and Los Angeles, California, and in Houston and Dallas, Texas, each with its own design head. The work itself is divided into three sections – landscape architecture, planning and urban design – with the scope of the last of these described as 'entire districts, as well as street systems, city blocks, waterfronts, parks, plazas and the smallest of urban areas'. Twenty-five per cent of SWA's work is now in China, and it has expanded into Russia and Mexico.

Gerdo Aquino, the new president of SWA, is also the co-author of a new book about the firm's work, *Landscape Infrastructure*, which positions it within the metaphorical framework of landscape urbanism. A summary of the book issued by SWA reveals something of the company's own current preoccupations: 'Infrastructure, as we know it, no longer belongs in the exclusive realm of engineers and transportation planners. In the context of our rapidly changing cities and towns, infrastructure is experiencing a paradigm shift where multiple-use programming and the integration of latent ecologies is a primary consideration. Defining contemporary infrastructure requires a multi-disciplinary team of landscape architects, engineers, architects and planners to fully realize the benefits to our cultural and natural systems.'

01

01-03 SWA's green roof for the California Academy
of Sciences features seven hillocks to echo
San Francisco's seven hills, positioned
around a central rectangular light well and
transparent roof for the internal piazza,
three storeys below.

For the Renzo Piano-designed California Academy of Sciences (2008), in San Francisco, SWA co-designed a 1-hectare (2.5-acre) green roof, together with horticultural consultant Paul Kephart of Rana Creek Living Architecture. The roof's contours conform to the facilities, offices and exhibition halls below, rising above the planetarium and the rainforest exhibit and lowering at the central piazza to introduce light and air into the heart of the building. The piazza is partly covered with glass to create a microclimate, enabling year-round use. Energy-efficient heating and cooling was integrated into the scheme, as were green building materials, minimal site disturbance, seasonal irrigation and energy generation. The roof is designed to thrive on natural, rather than mechanical, irrigation sources, and the drainage system recycles all storm-water run-off back into the water table. Photovoltaic cells line the roof perimeter, collecting solar energy to help power the building. As per Piano's original concept drawing, the roof's seven hills are intended to echo the seven major hills of San Francisco. Plants are first sown in trays off-site; when established, trucks outfitted with special racks transfer them to site. The plant trays, each containing three native species of grass, are then hoisted atop the roof and laid by hand over insulating and waterproofing materials inside the gabion channel grid. The trays also provide their own temporary support structure until the plants become well established on the rooftop. Over time, the trays disintegrate and become part of the soil system.

The Lite-On Electronic Headquarters (2006), in Taipei, Taiwan, is another striking rooftop design, a 1-hectare (2.5-acre) space on the podium at the foot of the twenty-five-storey tower. SWA created a sustainable landscape of linear gardens, pools and sleek waterfalls inspired by the building's view of the Gee Long River. The green

04

05

06

07

04-07 The patterning on the sloped roof space of the Lite-On Electronic Headquarters in Taipei comprises linear gardens, pools and waterfalls. At the rear of the building, steps and a fountain feature descend to street level.

roof, the first of its kind to be envisioned and built by a private developer in Taipei, stores storm water and then reuses it for irrigation. The rooftop gardens slope from the second storey down to street level, emphasizing the expansive city and river views. In response to the area's heavy rains and periodic typhoons, the roof garden supports low-growing groundcover and shrubs that can survive high winds. The shallow soil layer provides roof insulation for the building without adding too much weight. Trees were planted on the ground level and in protected areas to allow for better root growth and anchoring. The sloped roof means that the drainage system is better equipped to handle torrential downpours. To the rear of the building, the podium garden slopes towards the boulevard, and a fountain feature begins to step with the incline. Long, linear planting beds, lawn panels and granite walkways highlight the river vista here. Halfway down the sloped garden, a light well opens to the sky and the granite walkways become pedestrian bridges across the well, providing views of the tropical almond grove below. Camphor tree orchards flank the garden on both sides, and palm trees serve as street trees along the boulevard edge.

TURENSCAPE

BEIJING, CHINA

One of the most exciting companies operating anywhere today,
consistently experimental and innovative.

Employing some five hundred professionals, Turenscape is one of the first and largest private architectural firms in China. The research interests of its founder, Kongjian Yu, now a visiting professor at Harvard's Graduate School of Design, include the theory and method of urban and landscape planning, the cultural aspects of landscape, and ecological infrastructure from the national to the regional and local scale. Strongly influenced by the theories of the late Ian McHarg, Yu defines landscape architecture as 'the art of survival'. He argues that the profession must 'bring value back to the vernacular of the land and the people, and lead the way in urban development by planning and designing an infrastructure of landscape and ecology'. In this way, he says, 'we create links between the land, people and our spirits'. Yu has formed a research team of more than thirty people, whose guiding principle is to establish landscape security patterns that are integrated into the infrastructure to safeguard ecological processes and cultural heritage, and to guide urban development plans.

The Zhongshan Shipyard Park (2001) in China's Guangdong province is on the 11-hectare (27-acre) site of a shipyard that was constructed in the 1950s and closed in 1999. The site included an existing lake (connected via the Qijiang River to the sea) with fluctuating water levels of up to 1.1m (3 ft 7 in) daily, unchecked trees and vegetation, and the ruins of docks, cranes, water towers and other machinery. To meet the challenge of the water levels, a network of bridges was constructed at various elevations and integrated with terraced planting beds, so that native weeds from the salt marsh could be grown. With regard to the rusting docks and related machinery, three approaches were taken to dramatize the spirit of the site artistically and ecologically:

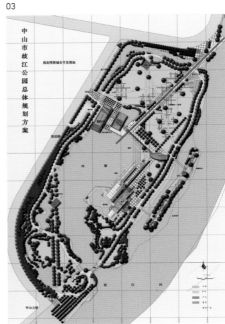

preservation; the modification of old forms; and the creation of new ones. The new forms included a network of straight paths, along with a red box and a green box that dramatized the character of the site. Dock buildings were restored for use as tea houses and club houses, accessible terraces were planted with native plants, a light tower was made from the former water storage facility, and paving was added under the trees. The park is now connected to the city via a network of paths and new facilities that include the restored tea houses, amenities that are both expected and appreciated in a Chinese park setting.

At Qinhuangdao, in Hebei, northern China, a new 26-hectare (64-acre) botanic garden (2009) was created on the site of a former tree nursery, the remains of which comprised seedlings, mature trees and a system road, as well as a number of small industrial buildings. Various existing trees were kept and integrated into the new design, including jujube (*Zizyphus jujuba*), purple vine (*Wisteria sinensis*), arborvitae (*Platycladus orientalis*) and pagoda trees (*Sophora japonica*), and the nursery's original path layout was retained. The new landscape was conceived as a series of distinct episodes inspired by the appearance of the landscape surroundings, with black bricks – a local vernacular material – used throughout. At one point an artificial valley cuts through an artificial mound (5m, or 16 ft, high), which displays the geological strata of the mountains of the region. Bridges have been placed on the top of the mound to allow people to have a frisson of the experience of walking above a valley. Other garden episodes include a series of four walled herb gardens, the jujube court, a perennial corridor that incorporates shade-providing metal sculptures, and the orchard fields, with peach, apple, pear, almond and walnut trees grown on terraces.

04

05

06–08 The Qinhuangdao botanic garden takes
the form of a series of varied episodes,
including the perennial walk with its giant
metal structures for shade, and a bridged
walkway that allows visitors to view an
evocation of the geological strata of the
nearby mountain range.

08

The design intention at the Tianjin Bridged
Gardens was to create a transitional space
between nature and the city. A continuous
red bridge links each hilled and sunken
garden, with a watchtower at each
intersection.

11

A major project for the company was the Tianjin Bridged Gardens (2008), set within a 50-hectare (123.5-acre) park between the northern coastal city of Tianjin and the manmade Qiao Yuan Park. The designers say that the site was deserted, heavily polluted and scattered with slum dwellings and temporary structures. The park and gardens were built simultaneously, with the landscape designed to improve water and soil conditions, create an environment that would celebrate the local culture and landscape, and provide recreational opportunities for the surrounding communities, numbering more than ten million residents. Yu and his team created a linear park that consisted of nine sunken gardens, ten hilled gardens and a waterfront, interconnected by an elevated path. The idea was to create a transitional space between the city and nature. The hilled gardens gradually slope from the city's edge down to the waterfront, where the pavement level reaches 5m (16 ft) above the water surface, allowing park users, especially the elderly and the disabled, easy access to the gardens and the sky-walk from the urban street. At the waterfront edge, cascading planters showcase different plant species, while the inclined stone walls relate to the different rocks excavated in the region. The sunken gardens were inspired by the local land patterns: water borders, crop fields, harvested farmlands, flowing rivers, marsh, meadow and pasture.

The landscape of the region is flat, and was once rich in wetlands and salt marshes that have since been destroyed by decades of urban development. It is difficult to grow trees in the native saline-alkali soil, so a thick layer of topsoil was needed to provide a stable base for trees, an approach widely used in the region. Uniformly raising the soil level, however, would have blocked the view to the waterfront from the city. The architects approached this problem by creating a series of 'windows' that 'cut' into the raised soil, creating a wave-like skyline. These windows allow views to the waterfront, but also open up views out to the natural landscape. The continuous red bridge links each hilled and sunken garden, with a watchtower at each intersection. This skywalk serves as both a connecting element and a linear observation platform, which places the observer in a line between the city and the park. It runs the length of the site, 5m (16 ft) above the main garden level, providing points of connection between the various small gardens and the rest of the park.

PATRICK VERBRUGGEN

BONHEIDEN, BELGIUM

Perfectly weighted minimalist design, conceived and executed for a loyal local clientele.

Practising as a self-employed 'garden architect' since 1986, Patrick Verbruggen specializes in perfectly weighted geometric designs at private residences, where expanses of turf play off the white walls of classic 'white-cube' Modernist houses. Water is usually a feature in these gardens, as are mature trees and shrubs (indeed, Verbruggen says he will generally retain mature specimens as valuable additions to any garden). The aim is to create a rationalistic yet idealized domestic paradise. Verbruggen states that the garden in such situations must interact with and respond to the house, because of the large volumes of glass that are typically incorporated in the main elevations. Every element of his designs, therefore, must work in conjunction with the views out from the house. This is not a designer who works 'on plan' first, placing spatiality at a premium; rather, he configures the design around the vistas.

Because he uses an edited-down vocabulary of plants and other features, Verbruggen's designs are ostensibly simple, but the designer explains that he intends all of his gardens to evolve and change over time, providing satisfaction for the owners. His designs are intended to reflect the changing seasons, above all. The inference is that seasonal variation will be made more manifest in gardens such as these, where there is little self-conscious ornamentation on show, and where a sense (even if just a memory) of the surrounding topgraphy is allowed to impinge on the garden's presiding tone or sensibility. As Verbruggen states: 'The atmosphere of a calm and serene garden must focus on space, light and shadow, the seasons and the countryside.'

The 8-hectare (20-acre) landscape at the Descamps residence (2007) at Sterrebeek, a suburb of Brussels, was made around a house designed by local architect Bruno

01 The Descamps residence, located outside
Brussels, is a prime example of Verbruggen's
method of integrating house with garden by
means of vistas.

02–05 A characteristically pared-down vocabulary
of materials distinguishes the Descamps
garden, which features a pool adjacent to
the kitchen area.

06–07 Views out into the agricultural landscape
directed the design of the garden at the
Gooris residence, in the Belgian village of
Lot. The sloping lawn complements the
geometric rationality of the architecture.

06

07

Erpicum, with whom Verbruggen worked closely from the earliest stages. In this case, the garden was, in fact, constructed before the house. A variety of hard materials were chosen, from the granite cobbles used for the entrance way to the hardwood decks on two sides of the building. The pool, which abuts the glass walls of the kitchen, makes it into 'a real island experience', according to the designer.

The Gooris residence (2005) in the village of Lot, Belgium, benefits from a fine view of fields, meadows and hedges, which formed the basis of Verbruggen's design. The living space and balcony-terrace are situated on the upper level of the house, providing views across the expansive, sloping lawn – an intimation of the 18th-century Picturesque movement, which has been found to complement Modernist architecture so well – and into the landscape beyond, where horses and cattle graze. The pool is the property's lowest point, its edges flush with the lawn and garden adjacent.

08-09 At another garden in Sterrebeek, the Peremans residence, Verbruggen introduced the bold move of a 'cut', lined with concrete walls, which links the lower ground level with the garden above. A mirror pool can be traversed on stepping stones.

09

At the Peremans residence (2002), located like the Descamps house in Sterrebeek, Verbruggen was dealing with a narrow plot (19m, or 62 ft), relative to the size of the house, and a sharp change in level across its length. His necessarily linear design incorporated a concrete-walled cut, 23m (75 ft) in length and filled with a small terrace and a mirror pond with stepping-stone slabs across it. At the upper level is a grass terrace that connects with the living room and kitchen level, while at the lower ground level the clients can use a 'wellness centre'.

WETTE + KÜNECKE

GÖTTINGEN, GERMANY

Classical German Modernism made relevant and updated
to a 21st-century milieu.

The firm, founded in 1994 by Wolfgang Wette, now employs five other landscape architects. (A sister company, Wette + Gödecke, formed in 2001 with Henning Gödecke, specializes in landscape planning.) Most of the company's work is in the states of Lower Saxony, Hesse and Thuringia, primarily with public authorities and companies. They are candid about the strengths of the lead partners: Wette is more interested in design, often inspired by the visual arts, while Ulrich Künecke (who joined in 2002) covers the durability and suitability of materials, and project management. Another member of the team is interested in the ancient practice of feng shui, and this also comes into play in their designs. The firm considers the transformation of parkland to be a key area of expertise, especially in the sphere of historic gardens. 'In retrospect, it is compelling to find to what extent design concepts are interlaced and associated with social, philosophical and political aspects,' they say. 'Our approach is governed by a historical analysis of garden design to answer the question: how can historic structures be accentuated in the context of modern garden design?'

The Grüne Mitte (2007), or 'green middle', represented Wette + Künecke's rehabilitation of an 81-hectare (200-acre) park that stands between the blocks of a former barracks site, made redundant in 1994, in the university town of Göttingen. The barracks blocks have been made into attractive apartments, but in the interim period the park between them had become completely overgrown. Inspired by their walks around the site and an appreciation of the special quality of light above the Leine River, the designers decided to retain something of that wild character in their scheme, relying on grass, wildflower meadows and the planting of orange-fruiting wild service trees.

01-03 The Grüne Mitte park stands between the residential blocks of a former barracks site in Göttingen. The red steel structures strike an artificial note in the midst of a naturalistic aesthetic across the park's 81 hectares (200 acres).

01

02

03

04-06 At the remains of Frauenberg Abbey, in Nordhausen, the designers imaginatively 'reconstructed' the bomb-damaged church, using a Corten steel frame and blue-glass 'garden'.

The continuing flux of nature visible in the new park was intended to refer in part to the 'evolution' of the barracks into apartments. Bright-red steel sculptures and long benches form focal points and brighten up the park on dull days. A sunken stainless-steel ball, which children like to play on, refers to the semicircular aesthetic of one of the primary red sculptures. Now the designers want the farther reaches of the park to grow even wilder, so that children can enjoy playing in them all the more.

The town of Nordhausen in eastern Germany was almost razed to the ground by Allied bombing in 1945; there was a concentration camp on the outskirts of town that provided the workforce for a V-2 rocket factory. Frauenberg Abbey (2006), a Cistercian monastery, was badly damaged in the raids and the building was subsequently partially rebuilt within the purlieu of the cloisters. Wette + Künecke won the competition for the redesign of the environs of the abbey, visualizing a design that did not attempt to reconstruct the building with stone and other older materials, but with steel and glass, as if to herald a new era of peace and to make reference to the ancient tradition of glass and metalwork at the church. The tall steel structure also evokes the scale of the original building. In addition, the 'garden' area of the abbey was not envisioned as a 'monastic herb garden', as cliché would dictate. A surface of blue-glass chips leads to a surviving doorway, suggesting a pool of water.

05

06

KIM WILKIE

RICHMOND, ENGLAND

Quietly visionary landscape architect, whose work is infused with deep thought and reflection; a specialist in elegant landform.

Kim Wilkie is a landscape architect with a sound historical grounding, who is as at home working on large-scale restorations as he is creating turf landforms that can be categorized as 'land art'. His designs, he says, are 'inspired by both memory and imagination'. Having studied history at Oxford and environmental design at the University of California, Berkeley, he set up his landscape studio in London in 1989. His recent work includes the creation of a courtyard garden at the Victoria & Albert Museum, London, the restoration of the 20th-century sculpture garden at Villa La Pietra, in Florence, and land sculptures at Heveningham Hall, Suffolk, and Shawford Park, Hampshire. On a large scale, he has been involved with the Thames Landscape Strategy in West London for more than a decade, improving the riverside experience and opening up important vistas back to the city.

At a private residence in Hampshire (2008), Wilkie created one of his signature amphitheatrical landforms. Superficially these bear a resemblance to the 18th-century terraces of Charles Bridgeman (at Claremont in Surrey, for example), whom Wilkie has described as his favourite designer. But his own interventions are unmistakably contemporary, not historical pastiche, since they have an abstract, unbounded quality that makes them appear almost natural in situ. Here, the 17th-century house had been tucked into the lee of a south-west ridge, leaving the garden cramped, with a rather chaotic slope looming over the south-facing rooms. The aim was to open up the space to form curving grass tiers that descend to a central zig-zag spine, allowing for easy access up and down. Wilkie points out that the hard northern light and frequent frost of England makes it particularly suitable for turf landforms such as these.

01-03 An awkward garden site in Hampshire has been given a sense of purpose by this unifying treatment. The house is well sited within its green landscape, and now has a transcendent aspect of abstraction.

01
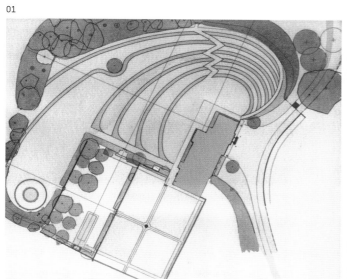

02

03

Boughton House (2010), in Northamptonshire, is one of Britain's greatest surviving formal landscape gardens, and features a rare 'canalscape' of linked waterways, rather than a single stretch of water as the centrepiece. Wilkie was all too aware of this when he was asked by the 9th Duke of Buccleuch to think about a feature that would have the strength to complement a garden design conceived on such a massive scale. His solution was Orpheus, a landform that mingles geometric clarity with mythic transcendence, though he says it is not necessary for visitors to understand the symbolism in order to enjoy it. Wilkie came up with the sunken design in response to the Duke's desire to create a landscape feature on an unused area of grass opposite a pyramidal mount, situated across one of the formal canals. The mount, believed to have been created by Bridgeman in 1724 (when it would have been the height of fashion), is tucked into an H-shaped section of the canal system, while the space in question was essentially a blank canvas of flat grassland until work began in 2007.

Wilkie's basic plan was to create a sunken mirror image of it, but going down instead of up, reversing the form to create a 'Hades' to complement the 'Olympus'

04-05 The Orpheus landform at Boughton House was integrated into an important historic formal landscape. The sunken feature is a mirror image of the 18th-century pyramidal mound on the opposite side of the canal.

represented by the mount. Visitors wandering the estate will not see the sunken space until they are almost upon it, though the steel-frame cube adjacent might alert them to the fact something extraordinary is coming up. A wide, shallow, grassy path leads inexorably down 7m (23 ft) to terminate in a dark, still square of water; here, there is a palpable sense of stillness and privacy. Meanwhile, up at ground level, a spiralling rill swirls around a rectangle etched into the ground, expressive of the perfect proportions of the Golden Section: the rectangle illustrated by the Roman architect, Vitruvius, which forms the basis for all classical and neoclassical architecture and underlying the compositional structure of numerous great Renaissance paintings. Wilkie says that the Orpheus myth came to mind following his initial impulse to create a subterranean feature. Orpheus is associated with the underworld because he descended there in order to rescue his lover, Eurydice, who had been killed by a snake. His music-making so delighted Hades that Eurydice was given the chance to follow Orpheus out of the underworld, and thus come back to life, on one condition: that Orpheus never looked back. This being Greek myth, it is not difficult to guess what happened next.

05

WIRTZ INTERNATIONAL

SCHOTEN, BELGIUM

Father-and-son team recognized worldwide for their beautifully pared-down landscape vocabulary of hedges, canals and topiary.

A Wirtz garden is an unmistakable and unforgettable sight, a modern reworking of the canals, lawns and topiary familiar from the vocabulary of classical garden and landscape design in the Low Countries. The vast majority of Jacques and Peter Wirtz's work has been completed in Belgium and the Netherlands, though recently they have been working elsewhere, including the USA and England, where they provided a masterplan for the ambitious redesign of the walled garden at Alnwick Castle, Northumberland. Though well known for their tranquil, minimalist private gardens, the duo are as comfortable working for corporate or public clients on a much larger scale. The firm prides itself on a pragmatic approach to landscape design and especially horticulture. Of particular importance is what they call 'a constant preoccupation with the relationship of the human figure's scale and its surrounding landscape'.

The private garden pictured opposite is a typical Wirtz design, with beautifully cloud-pruned box hedges backed by fruit trees, raising the entire effect of the space through the apparently simplest of means. The structure of the garden, a former vegetable plot, is based on criss-crossing paths. The beds contain nursery stock and experimental plants.

In the historic centre of Bruges, the Van Damm garden is a remarkable space conceived as an outdoor gallery for its art-collector owners. A raised, rectilinear-shaped pond, surrounded by a box, reflects the water into an adjacent greenhouse; from the pond, box hedges swirl round existing yew trees to give depth to the garden. The design of hedges, a pool and mature trees is visually complex and most effective. 'This more contemporary form, in combination with the rectangular shape of the

garden, provides an interesting symbiosis of shapes,' the Wirtzes say. 'The curving geometries create spaces to implement the art. Even in winter, when the sky is grey, the light green of the hedges and the reflecting water of the pond make the garden look bright.'

The Coolsaet estate is in the grounds of a large model farm, north of Antwerp, the land of which is subdivided into parcels defined by beech and chestnut trees. The project involved the landscaping of an existing courtyard with swimming pool and a principal vista from one façade of the house, across former grazing pastures. The courtyard was subdivided as a formal iris and box garden, with a perennial border and an area of ornamental grasses surrounded by wood trellis that screens the pool. The main vista terminates at an asymmetric space in one corner of the estate, in the shadow of a line of old beech trees. To counter this asymmetry, the Wirtzes expressed the axial dimension of the view by means of a sequence of mirror ponds in an inversed forced

03

04

01 Cloud-pruned box hedges are often used by the Wirtzes in their designs, here in a private garden with fruit trees defining the cross-axis structure.
02 The Van Damm garden in the heart of Bruges exhibits the Wirtzes' versatility as designers, for it is a small space with a specific purpose as an outdoor art gallery.
03-04 At the Coolsaet estate, near Antwerp, the Wirtzes redesigned an existing large garden, creating a formal box-hedged iris garden and a principal view from the house, emphasized by a series of mirror pools along its length.

perspective, ending on a raised platform with a circle of cherries and columnar oaks. One oak at the pasture's former boundary has been left in the view, creating a pleasant tension, the designers say, 'as if nature was rebelling against the design'.

Sibelco, an extractor of sand and materials, is the owner of an old sand quarry, now filled with water and turned into a nature reserve. The company decided to restore the ancient farmhouse into a museum, turning the entire site into a semi-public park where people can enjoy the lake and its edge. As the soil is extremely sandy, the Wirtzes chose simply to introduce uniform sweeps of the grass *Miscanthus sinensis* to create a natural look and a feel of movement. The structure of these grasses lasts throughout the winter.

05

06

07

08

05-08 Sometimes the simplest of means can be the
most effective. At the Sibelco sand quarry
and museum, the Wirtzes used just one
plant, miscanthus grass, to create an abiding
atmosphere appropriate to the place.

ZUS

ROTTERDAM, NETHERLANDS

A funky and unpredictable company that eschews the bijou,
envisaging fantastical work on a large scale.

ZUS (Zones Urbaines Sensibles) was founded in 2001 in Rotterdam by Elma van Boxel
and Kristian Koreman, who happily produce both commissioned and unsolicited
designs and research studies in the fields of architecture, urbanism and landscape
design. Happily, because research is genuinely a large part of their office's stated remit.
They are particularly energetic in the field of 'urban politics', believing in the role of
landscape architects as political and cultural activists. In this they have proved an
inspiration to many of their contemporaries. The firm employs four more architects
and one landscape architect, in addition to the principals.

Almere is a new city (established in 1976) in the northwestern corner of the
Netherlands. The Almere Duin project is ZUS's response to the need for a coastal-
landscape strategy for the city, with the concept of dunes as the underlying idea. ZUS's
plan calls for three artificial dunes to be created along the edge of a principal dyke in
the wilderness where Almere gives way to the sea, on either side of the city. Wooded
areas will alternate with small settlements and a central valley feature, which will be
filled with pink magnolias and traversed by boardwalks, creating a variety of habitats.
ZUS's plan is for the dunescape to appear as a mirage to local residents as they emerge
from the high-rise office buildings and programmatic residential developments. The
city authority and a private investor have agreed on a thirty-year plan that ZUS hopes
will mean the project will develop at the correct speed.

One of ZUS's more outlandish hypothetical landscape studies is its idea for a
glass-enclosed '6th Avenue', a strip of hotels, shops and entertainment facilities that
will run from Schiphol Airport to Amsterdam's harbour area. Their plan is for this

01-02 ZUS's bold idea for Almere is a
redevelopment based on the idea of
three artificial dunes. The firm envisages
the project as a fruitful contrast to the
'Modernist utopia' of the rest of city.

03-04 '6th Avenue' is an idea for a long, glass-
       walled passageway that will run from
       Schiphol Airport to the harbour. The space
       created will provide opportunities for a huge
       range of retail and leisure facilities.

long passageway to be split in two along its entire length – the 'air' side and the 'land' side, as in any conventional airport terminal. ZUS argues that the sheer scale of what they propose will produce a more authentic and useful experience for visitors and residents. As they put it: 'The strip becomes a large terminal, which combines authentic leisure landscapes with the product-orientated seduction machine.'

Not many landscape firms have an 'urban politics' work category, but ZUS has issued a number of manifestos as part of its output. One of the most bracing is the 'Letter to the Minister' (2007), addressed to the new Minister of Transport, Spatial Planning and the Environment, arguing for a coherent long-term planning policy that might outlast several government administrations, rather than the piecemeal approach common throughout the developed world. Some extracts from the letter:

'The motto "local if possible, central if unavoidable" created a Netherlands dominated by a succession of fiercely competitive business parks and suburban residential utopias. The south side of the Randstad seems to have served as the prototype for the most recent policy documents: an illegible, complex urban tapestry, showing clearly that we cannot entrust the public interest of cultural-historical landscapes, townscapes and the need for control to local authorities and their project developers and urban designers. Our proposal is as simple as it is effective. The large amount of water-storage area that will have to be provided in the coming years, estimated at 7,500 hectares [18,533 acres], should be divided between existing towns and villages. A water margin laid round each core would define its territory, forming, as it were, a moat. Urban cores would be urged to treat the available space innovatively, so that areas that become empty would be given a new use. Even the edge of the town would become valuable, because it would offer an exclusive view of the countryside. It would therefore automatically attract more attention than at present, when such areas are often referred to as the "edge of town".'

Such missives issued by ZUS operate somewhere between satire and practical prescription.

Directory

Contributor biographies:
Critics and designers' forums

Further reading

Picture credits

DIRECTORY

Agence TER [10]

35, rue des 3 Bornes
75011 Paris
France
+33 1 43 14 34 00
contact@agenceter.com
Hübschstraße 19 D
76135 Karlsruhe
Germany
+49 721 81 98 97 20
mail@agenceter.de
48, avenue de Monnerville
97374 Kourou
French Guiana
+33 594 32 43 09
ter.gf@wanadoo.fr
www.agenceter.com

Balmori [18]

833 Washington Street, 2nd floor
New York, New York 10014
USA
+1 (212) 431-9191
info@balmori.com
www.balmori.com

Patrick Blanc [22]

France
contact@murvegetalpatrickblanc.com
www.murvegetalpatrickblanc.com

Christopher Bradley-Hole [26]

Greystone House, Sudbrook Lane
Richmond TW1Q 7AT
UK
+44 20 8939 1748
info@christopherbradley-hole.co.uk
www.christopherbradley-hole.co.uk

Bruto [32]

Mesarska 4d
1000 Ljubljana
Slovenia
+ 386 1 232 21 95
matej.kucina@bruto.si
www.bruto.si

Fernando Caruncho [38]

Antonio Maura 16, 3rd floor
28014 Madrid
Spain
+34 91 532 10 49
info@fernandocaruncho.com
www.fernandocaruncho.com

Andrea Cochran [46]

2325 Third Street, #210
San Francisco, California 94107
USA
+1 (415) 503-0060
acla@acochran.com
www.acochran.com

Vladimir Djurovic [52]

Villa Rizk Broumana
Lebanon
+961 4 862 444
info@vladimirdjurovic.com
www.vladimirdjurovic.com

estudioOCA [56]

1737 Whitley Avenue, #307
Los Angeles, California 90028
USA
+1 (323) 405-7436
losangeles@estudiooca.com
1429 Kearny Street, #1
San Francisco, California 94133
USA
+1 (415) 240-4896
sanfrancisco@estudiooca.com
Travessera de Dalt, 21–23, 5º 2ª
08024 Barcelona
Spain
+34 931 813 945
barcelona@estudiooca.com
27, rue des Frères Pecchini
13007 Marseille
France
+33 486 77 48 82
marseille@estudiooca.com
470, rue Khalleb, quartier Issil, 4
40000 Marrakech
Morocco
+212 524 30 95 83
marrakech@estudiooca.com
Rua Jesuíno Arruda, 122 ap 151 C
04532–080 Itaim Bibi, São Paulo
Brazil
+55 11 9316 7439
saopaulo@estudiooca.com
www.estudiooca.com

Formwerkz [70]

12 Prince Edward Road
Bestway Building
Annex D 01-01/02
Singapore 079212
+65 644 00 551
admin@formwerkz.com
www.formwerkz.com

GREENinc [76]

83 Sixth Street
Parkhurst, Johannesburg
South Africa
+27 11 327 3687
admin@greeninc.co.za
www.greeninc.co.za

Juan Grimm [84]

Zurich 221 Of. 12
Las Condes, Santiago
Chile
+56 2 234 1245
juangrimm@juangrimm.cl
www.juangrimm.cl

Hager [90]

Bergstraße 85
8032 Zurich
Switzerland
+41 44 266 3030
info@hager-ag.ch
www.hager-ag.ch

Hocker Design Group [96]

918 Dragon Street
Dallas, Texas 75207
USA
+1 (214) 915-0910
info@hockerdesign.com
www.hockerdesign.com

Hoerr Schaudt [102]

850 West Jackson Boulevard, Suite 800
Chicago, Illinois 60607
USA
+1 (312) 492-6501
www.hoerrschaudt.com

Hood Design [106]

3016 Filbert Street, #2
Oakland, California 94608
USA
+1 (510) 595-0688
walter@wjhooddesign.com
www.wjhooddesign.com

Charles Jencks [110]

London, UK
www.charlesjencks.com

Mikyoung Kim [126]

119 Braintree Street, Suite 103
Boston, Massachusetts 02134
USA
+1 (617) 782-9130
office@mikyoungkim.com
www.mikyoungkim.com

Landscape India [132]

901 Panchtirth, Opp. Aristroville
Satellite Road
Ahmedabad 380015
India
+91 79 2692 0554
landscapeindia@usa.net
www.landscapeindia.net

Latz + Partner [138]

Ampertshausen 6
D-85402 Kranzberg
Germany
+49 81 66 67 85 0
post@latzundpartner.de
Studio 1A, Highgate Business Centre
33 Greenwood Place
London NW5 1LB
UK
+44 20 7482 6320
london@latzundpartner.de
www.latzundpartner.de

Tom Leader [144]

1015 Camelia Street
Berkeley, California 94710
USA
+1 (510) 524-3363
mail@tomleader.com
www.tomleader.com

Levin Monsigny [148]

Brunnenstraße 181
10119 Berlin
Germany
+49 30 4405 3184
mail@levin-monsigny.com
www.levin-monsigny.com

Lohaus Carl [152]

Lister Meile 33
30161 Hanover
Germany
+49 511 33 65 49 60
info@lohaus.carl.de
www.lohauscarl.de

McGregor Coxall [156]

21c Whistler Street
Manly, New South Wales
Australia
+61 2 9977 3853
www.mcgregorcoxall.com

Mesa Design Group [162]

1807 Ross Avenue, Suite 333
Dallas, Texas 75201
USA
+1 (214) 871-0568
C. Claudio Coello, 28 – 3º Der.
28001 Madrid
Spain
+34 917 454 185
Holiday Centre, Sheikh Zayed Road
Dubai
United Arab Emirates
+971 4 311 7176
RBS Building
Hamdan Street, Suite 303/1–2
Abu Dhabi
United Arab Emirates
+971 2 678 8069
www.mesadesigngroup.com

Teresa Moller [170]

Av. Luis Pasteur 5687
Vitacura, Santiago
Chile
+56 218 3116
www.teresamoller.cl

N-Tree [174]

1-25-32 Naitou
Kokubunji-shi
Tokyo 185-0033
Japan
info@n-tree.jp
www.n-tree.jp

OAB [178]

Corsega 254 Bajos
08008 Barcelona
Spain
+34 93 238 51 36
oab@ferrater.com
www.ferrater.com

The Office of James Burnett [194]

550 Lomas Santa Fe, Suite A
Solana Beach, California 92075
USA
+1 (858) 793-6970
3313 D'Amico Avenue
Houston, Texas 77019
USA
+1 (713) 529-9919
marketing@ojb.com
www.ojb.com

Ossart & Maurières [200]

2, rue Henry Drussy
41000 Blois
France
+33 2 54 55 06 37

Piet Oudolf [206]

Broekstraat 17
6999 Hummelo
Netherlands
www.oudolf.com

Dan Pearson [214]

The Nursery, The Chandlery
50 Westminster Bridge Road
London SE1 7QY
UK
+44 20 7928 3800
www.danpearsonstudio.com

Péna & Peña Paysages [222]

15, rue Jean Fautrier
75013 Paris
France
+33 1 45 70 00 80
Le Serre d'Aubrias
07140 Malbosc
France
+33 4 75 36 92 33
contact@penapaysages.com
www.penapaysages.com

Planergruppe Oberhausen [228]

Lothringerstraße 21
46045 Oberhausen
Germany
+49 208 880 550
info@planergruppe-oberhausen.de
www.planergruppe-oberhausen.de

POLA [232]

Neue Schönhauserstraße, 16
10178 Berlin
Germany
+49 30 240 834 15
mail@pola-berlin.de
www.pola-berlin.de

Patricia Pozzi [236]

via Paolo Frisi, 3
20129 Milan
Italy
+39 2 76 00 39 12
landscape@patriziapozzi.it
www.patriziapozzi.it

Proap [250]

Lisbon
Portugal
www.proap.pt

Raderschall Partner [258]

Burgstraße 69
8706 Meilen
Switzerland
+41 44 925 55 00
info@raderschall.ch
www.raderschall.ch

Sant en Co [264]

1e Sweelinckstraat 72
2517 The Hague
Netherlands
+41 70 346 37 86
mail@santenco.nl
www.santenco.nl

The Sheffield School [268]

James Hitchmough
Department of Landscape
University of Sheffield
UK
+44 114 222 0610
j.d.hitchmough@sheffield.ac.uk
www.landscape.dept.shef.ac.uk/james

Nigel Dunnett
Department of Landscape
University of Sheffield
UK
+44 114 222 0611
+44 7716 996 696
n.dunnett@sheffield.ac.uk
www.nigeldunnett.info

Noël Kingsbury
Montpelier Cottage
Brilley, Herefordshire HR3 6HF
UK
+44 1497 831189
noel@noelkingsbury.com
www.noelkingsbury.com

Stephen Stimson [276]

15 Depot Avenue
Falmouth, Massachusetts 02540
USA
+1 (508) 548-8119
288 Norfolk Street
Cambridge, Massachusetts 02139
USA
+1 (617) 876-8960
mail@stephenstimson.com
www.stephenstimson.com

Tom Stuart-Smith [282]

Greenhill House
90/93 Cowcross Street
London EC1M 6BF
UK
+44 20 7253 2100
info@tomstuartsmith.co.uk
www.tomstuartsmith.co.uk

Surface Design [288]

131 Lower Terrace
San Francisco, California 94114
USA
360 North Sepulveda Boulevard
Suite 3060
El Segundo, California 90245
USA
+1 (415) 621-5522
info@sdisf.com
www.sdisf.com

SWA Group [306]

2200 Bridgeway Boulevard
Sausalito, California 94966
USA
+1 (415) 332-5100
sausalito@swagroup.com
580 Broadway Beach
Laguna Beach, California 92651
laguna@swagroup.com
1245 West 18th Street
Houston, Texas 77008
USA
+1 (713) 868-1676
houston@swagroup.com
2211 North Lamar, Suite 400
Dallas, Texas 75202
USA
+1 (214) 954-0016
dallas@swagroup.com
55 New Montgomery, Suite 888
San Francisco, California 94105
USA
+1 (415) 836-8770
sanfrancisco@swagroup.com
811 West 7th Street, Suite 430
Los Angeles, California 90017
USA
+1 (213) 236-9090
losangeles@swagroup.com
V10 14F, Jinjiang Xiangyang Building
No. 993 Najing West Road
Shanghai 200041
China
+86 21 3217 0603
shanghai@swagroup.com
www.swagroup.com

Turenscape [312]

Room 401, Innovation Centre
Peking University Science Park
127–1, Zhongguancun North Street
Haidian District, Beijing 100080
China
+86 10 6296 7408
info@turenscape.com
www.turenscape.com

Patrick Verbruggen [320]

Hondshoek 58
2820 Bonheiden
Belgium
+32 15 331 433
patrick.verbruggen3@pandora.be
www.patrickverbruggen.be

Wette + Künecke [326]

Kehrstraße 12a
37085 Göttingen
Germany
+49 551 79 20 80
www.wgk-planung.de

Kim Wilkie [330]

34 Friars' Stile Road
Richmond TW10 6NE
UK
+44 20 8332 0304
info@kimwilkie.com
www.kimwilkie.com

Wirtz International [334]

Botermelkdijk 464
2900 Schoten
Belgium
+32 3 680 13 22
info@wirtznv.be
www.wirtznv.be

ZUS [340]

Schiekade 189
P.O. Box 2024
3000 Rotterdam
Netherlands
+31 10 233 9409
info@zus.ccw
www.zus.cc

CONTRIBUTOR BIOGRAPHIES:
CRITICS & DESIGNERS' FORUM

Lodewijk Baljon graduated from Wageningen University and received his PhD in 1992. Since 1986 he has based his office in Amsterdam, where he works with a team of ten designers on a variety of private and public projects that range from landscape architecture to urban design. The design work is supported by teaching, research and writing. He has been the recipient of the most prestigious prize for urban design in the Netherlands, the OmgevingsArchitectuurPrijs. In 2004 Baljon received two awards from the American Society of Landscape Architects. Recently he has been awarded the Dutch Design Award (public space); the German Design Prize for the Station Square in Apeldoorn; and the National Building Prize (integral design) for the urban gardens at the government office complex in Groningen. Baljon has written numerous critical essays on urban and landscape developments and lectures on a regular basis, and has also taught at Harvard's Graduate School of Design.

Gilles Clément spent his childhood in Algeria and the Creuse, south of Paris, where his famous garden La Vallée later evolved. He was a conscientious objector in Nicaragua, then gained degrees in both agronomy and landscape architecture, the latter at the École Nationale Supérieure du Paysage de Versailles, where he now teaches. As a designer, he undertakes both private and public projects, such as the Parc Citroën and Musée Branly gardens, both in Paris, the Domaine du Rayol on France's south coast, and the Abbaye de Valloires, in Picardy. He is also highly regarded as the author of numerous essays and novels. His most famous 'idea-tools' to date are the 'Moving Garden' (the gardener participates in the natural dynamic), the 'Planetary Garden' (caring for the earth as for a garden), 'Landscapes of the Third Kind' (the forgotten spaces between managed land, the rich in biodiversity) and 'Symbiotic Man.' His current design projects are in an ecological utopia in southern Morocco, Tahiti, Libya, deepest rural France, and elsewhere. Clément has become more militant in recent years; his Nettle Garden at Melle was created as a protest against restrictions on home remedies in organic gardening. He is currently creating a project on the Mexican–American border on the theme of migrating populations, plants and people.

Claude Cormier is a landscape architect and principal of Claude Cormier Architectes Paysagistes, in Montréal. Cormier studied history and theory of design at Harvard University, landscape architecture at the University of Toronto and agronomy at the University of Guelph. Establishing an office in Montréal in 1995, Cormier's internationally recognized practice extends far beyond the conventional realm of traditional landscape design to forge bridges between urban design, public art and architecture. Cormier has taught at the University of Montréal and has been invited to lecture across Canada, the United States and Europe. In 2009, Cormier was knighted with the Ordre national du Québec, the highest distinction bestowed by the government of the province.

Kate Cullity is a principal of Taylor Cullity Lethlean, with offices in Melbourne and Adelaide. The firm undertakes investigations into the poetic expression of the Australian landscape and contemporary culture, an approach that permeates its design work in a multiplicity of public settings, from urban waterfronts to desert walking trails. In each case, the detailed exploration of context, site and community have informed outcomes and enriched the patterning and detail of built landscapes. Four streams of investigation have informed the practice's work: contemporary urban life and global culture; the elemental power of site and landscape; artistic practice in a range of disciplines; and the creation of a sustainable future. Many projects have been for significant cultural institutions, such as museums, botanic gardens, universities and national parks, while others have been part of major urban redevelopments. Cullity and her colleagues, Kevin Taylor and Perry Lethlean, each bring different disciplines and skills to the firm. Along with a shared background in landscape architecture, Taylor is trained in architecture, Cullity in botany and the visual arts, and Lethlean in urban design. The practice's designs have often arisen from collaboration with fellow designers and artists, resulting in the creation of memorable environments characterized by the achievement of a shared vision and the sensitive integration of buildings, artworks and landscape. The results of a dynamic dialogue with clients, communities, academics and colleagues is an eclectic body of work woven together by a common thread of quality, commitment and surprisingly simple yet rich environments that support the life of the communities they serve.

Penelope Hobhouse is an internationally respected garden designer and historian based in Somerset. She is well known for the creation of the garden at Tintinhull House in Somerset, and for her books, which include *Plants in Garden History* and *The Gardens of Persia*.

Louisa Jones grew up in Nova Scotia, in a family of naturalists and writers. She studied in France and the United States before getting a doctorate in French literature. While professor at the University of Washington in Seattle, she published books on pastoral art and literature and was invited to speak at a symposium on Watteau at the Louvre (1985) and began teaching American students in Provence. In 1975, she and her husband settled on a terraced hillside in the southern Rhône valley, where they began hands-on gardening and where they still live. After visiting some two hundred gardens of all kinds in Provence, Jones published her first book, *Gardens in Provence* (1992), which linked gardens, social history and landscape. Twenty-nine other books have followed in French or English, based on personal visits and research, including *Kitchen Gardens of France*, *The French Country Garden*, a history of the Chaumont festival, and two books with ecologist Gilles Clément (see left). She lectures all over the world, and leads private visits to gardens in Provence. Jones's forthcoming books include *Nicole de Vésian: Un Art des Jardins en Provence*, *Manifeste pour les jardins méditerranéens* and *Mediterranean Landscape Art: The Vernacular Muse*.

Gavin Keeney is an author, editor and critic based in New York. His most recent book is *Art as 'Night': An Art-Theological Treatise* (2010).

Noël Kingsbury is well known internationally as a promoter of innovation in horticulture and landscape. His main interest is the development of planting design, based on a love and knowledge of wild plant communities. He has authored some twenty books, and is an associate of the department of landscape at the University of Sheffield, South Yorkshire.

Ron Lutsko is principal and founder of Lutsko Associates, a landscape architecture firm in San Francisco, California. The company's philosophy combines an interest in design, art and ecology to create contemporary landscapes connected to their ecological region. Lutsko was educated at the University of California, Davis, with degrees in landscape architecture and horticulture, and did his graduate work at the University of California, Berkeley, where he received his masters' degree in

Landscape Architecture. He went on to teach at both campuses and founded Lutsko Associates in 1981. Lutsko, with his wife and daughters, also run an organic farm, producing artisan olive oil. He has served on many boards and advisory committees related to public gardens, environmental education and organic farming.

Paolo Pejrone is Italy's most distinguished landscape architect. He has had a long and influential career designing private and public gardens and landscapes.

Martha Schwartz is a landscape architect and artist with a major interest in urban projects and the exploration of innovative design expression in the landscape. She has over thirty years of experience collaborating with world-renowned architects on a diverse portfolio of projects. As president of Martha Schwartz Partners, with offices in Cambridge, Massachusetts and London, England, she provides landscape-design solutions that enhance the social, environmental and economic sustainability of a place, and raises them to the level of fine art. Schwartz is currently a professor in Practice of Landscape Architecture at Harvard's Graduate School of Design. She is also the founder of the Harvard University Working Group for Sustainable Cities, through which she and her colleagues find solutions for urban sustainability issues. Schwartz has received numerous awards, including the 2006 Cooper-Hewitt Landscape Award for her body of work. She has lectured and been published worldwide.

Ken Smith is one of the best known of a new generation of landscape architects who are equally at home in the worlds of art, architecture and urbanism. Trained in both design and the fine arts, he explores the relationship between art, contemporary culture and landscape. His practice, Workshop: Ken Smith Landscape Architect, was established in 1992 and is based in New York with a Southern California office in Irvine. Smith's approach is directed at projects of varying scales and types: temporary installations, private residential gardens, public spaces, parks and commercial projects. With a particular emphasis on projects that explore the symbolic content and expressive power of landscape as an art form, the Workshop specializes in the investigation of new expressions in landscape design. Smith is a graduate of Iowa State University and Harvard's Graduate School of Design. He has taught and lectured at Harvard, the City College of New York, and at other universities and institutions around the world. Smith's work has been published widely in the popular and trade press.

Mario Terzic has been a professor at the University of Applied Arts, Vienna, and head of the master class for graphic arts since 1991. In 1998 he co-founded the Trinidad group of conceptual landscape design, which until 2004 produced a large number of plans for projects that united art, garden and agriculture. In 2000 he oversaw the foundation of the department for landscape design at the University of Applied Arts, which he currently heads.

Marc Treib is professor emeritus at the University of California, Berkeley, a practicing graphic designer and a noted landscape and architectural historian and critic. He has published widely on modern and historical subjects in the United States, Japan and Scandinavia, including *An Everyday Modernism: The Houses of William Wurster* (1995) and *Space Calculated in Seconds: The Philips Pavilion, Le Corbusier, Edgard Varèse* (1996). Recent books include *Noguchi in Paris: The UNESCO Garden* (2003); *Thomas Church, Landscape Architect: Designing a Modern California Landscape* (2004); *Settings and Stray Paths: Writings on Landscapes and Gardens* (2005); *Representing Landscape Architecture* (2007); *Drawing/Thinking: Confronting an Electronic Age* (2008); *Spatial Recall: Memory in Architecture and Landscape* (2009); and *Appropriate: The Houses of Joseph Esherick* (2009).

Bernard Tschumi is an architect based in New York and Paris. First known as a theorist, he exhibited and published *The Manhattan Transcripts* (1981) and *Architecture and Disjunction* (1994), a series of theoretical essays. In 1983 he won a prestigious competition to design and build the Parc de la Villette, in Paris. Since then, he has made a reputation for groundbreaking designs that include the new Acropolis Museum in Athens, Le Fresnoy centre for the contemporary arts, in Tourcoing, France, and the Vacheron Constantin corporate headquarters in Geneva, among other projects. Tschumi's work has been widely exhibited, with solo exhibitions at the Museum of Modern Art in New York and the Venice Biennale. He also served as dean of the Graduate School of Architecture, Planning and Preservation at Columbia University in New York (1988–2003).

Michael Van Valkenburgh is a principal of Michael Van Valkenburgh Associates, with offices in Brooklyn, New York, and in Cambridge, Massachusetts. Van Valkenburgh's work and teaching is known for emphasizing the experiential possibilities of the living landscape, and the potential for landscape methodologies to influence urban development in ways that promote social and environmental sustainability. Since 1982 he has taught at Harvard's Graduate School of Design, where he is currently a professor in Practice of Landscape Architecture. Van Valkenburgh was the recipient of the 2010 Arnold W. Brunner Memorial Prize in Architecture, and the 2003 National Design Award in Environmental Design awarded by the Cooper-Hewitt National Design Museum. Brooklyn Bridge Park, designed by Van Valkenburgh and several colleagues, was awarded the 2010 Brendan Gill Prize by the New York City Municipal Art Society.

Richard Weller is Winthrop Professor of Landscape Architecture at the University of Western Australia, where he is well known for combining teaching, research and practice. In over twenty-five years of design practice, Weller has received a stream of international design-competition awards. He has published over seventy papers and given hundreds of invited lectures around the world. His design work has been widely exhibited, including in a retrospective at the Museum of Contemporary Art in Sydney (1998), and published as a monograph by the University of Pennsylvania Press in 2005. Weller's recent planning work is *'Boomtown 2050': Scenarios for a Rapidly Growing City* (2009). His current research concerns urban growth scenarios to meet Australia's predicted mid-century population growth, and he is a lead consultant for the new waterfront development for the city of Perth.

FURTHER READING

Almy, Dean, ed., *Center 14: On Landscape Urbanism* (Austin: The Center for American Architecture and Design, University of Texas at Austin, 2007).

Amidon, Jane, *Ken Smith Landscape Architect: Urban Projects* (New York: Princeton Architectural Press, 2009).

Balmori, Diana, *A Landscape Manifesto* (New Haven, Connecticut: Yale University Press, 2010).

Berrizbeitia, Anita, ed., *Michael Van Valkenburgh Associates: Reconstructing Urban Landscapes* (New Haven, Connecticut: Yale University Press, 2009).

Blanc, Patrick, *The Vertical Garden: In Nature and the City* (London: W. W. Norton & Co, 2008).

Bradley-Hole, Christopher, *The Minimalist Garden* (London: Mitchell Beazley, 1999).

———, *Making the Modern Garden* (London: Mitchell Beazley, 2004).

Clément, Gilles, *Le Jardin en mouvement* (Paris: Sens & Tonka, 1991).

Cooper, Guy, and Gordon Taylor, *Mirrors of Paradise: The Gardens of Fernando Caruncho* (New York: Monacelli Press, 2000).

Corner, James, ed., *Recovering Landscape: Essays in Contemporary Landscape Theory* (New York: Princeton Architectural Press, 2000).

Czerniak, Julia, ed., *Downsview Park Toronto* (Munich: Prestel Verlag, 2001).

Dunnett, Nigel, and James Hitchmough, eds, *The Dynamic Landscape: Naturalistic Planting in an Urban Context* (London: Taylor & Francis, 2004).

Forman, Richard T. T., *Urban Regions: Ecology and Planning Beyond the City* (Cambridge, England: Cambridge University Press, 2008).

Goldsmith, Stephen A. and Lynne Elizabeth, eds, *What We See: Advancing the Observations of Jane Jacobs* (Oakland, California: A New Village Press), 2010.

Heathcote, Edwin, 'The Regeneration Game', in *The Financial Times*, December 11, 2010.

Hobhouse, Penelope, *The Story of Gardening* (London: Dorling Kindersley Publishers, 2002).

Jencks, Charles, *The Garden of Cosmic Speculation* (London: Frances Lincoln Publishers, 2003).

Jones, Louisa, *The Garden Visitor's Companion* (London: Thames & Hudson, 2009).

Koolhaas, Rem, and Bruce Mau, *S, M, L, XL* (New York: Monacelli Press, 1995).

Lehmann, Steffen, *The Principles of Green Urbanism: Transforming the City for Sustainability* (London: Taylor & Francis, 2010).

Mostafavi, Mohsen, and Gareth Doherty, eds, *Ecological Urbanism* (Baden, Switzerland: Lars Müller Publishers, 2010).

Mostafavi, Mohsen, and Ciro Najle, eds, *Landscape Urbanism: A Manual for the Machinic Landscape* (London: Architectural Association, 2003).

Myers, Mary, *Andrea Cochran: Landscapes* (New York: Princeton Architectural Press, 2009).

Monel, Yann, Gilles Le Scanff and Joëlle-Caroline Mayer, *Les Jardins de Ossart et Maurières* (Paris: Éditions du Chêne, 2008).

Oudolf, Piet, and Noël Kingsbury, *Designing with Plants* (London: Conran Octopus, 1999).

Pearson, Dan, *Spirit: Garden Inspiration* (London: FUEL Design & Publishing, 2009).

Pyla, Panayiota, 'Counter-Histories of Sustainability', in *Volume 18* (2008).

Richardson, Tim, *Avant Gardeners: 50 Visionaries of the Contemporary Landscape* (London: Thames & Hudson, 2008).

———, *English Gardens in the Twentieth Century: From the Archives of 'Country Life'* (London: Aurum Press, 2005).

———, *Great Gardens of America* (London: Frances Lincoln Publishers, 2009).

———, *The Vanguard Gardens and Landscapes of Martha Schwartz* (London: Thames & Hudson, 2004).

Richardson, Tim, and Noël Kingsbury, *Vista: The Culture and Politics of Gardens* (London: Frances Lincoln Publishers, 2005).

Rocca, Alessandro, ed., *Planetary Gardens: The Landscape Architecture of Gilles Clément* (Basel: Birkhäuser Verlag, 2009).

Rowe, Peter G., *Making a Middle Landscape* (Cambridge, Massachusetts: MIT Press, 1991).

Treib, Marc, ed., *Spatial Recall: Memory in Architecture and Landscape* (London: Routledge, 2009).

Trulove, James Grayson, ed., *Ten Landscapes: Stephen Stimson* (Gloucester, Massachusetts: Rockport Publishers, 2002).

Waldheim, Charles, ed., *The Landscape Urbanism Reader* (New York: Princeton Architectural Press, 2006).

Weilacher, Udo, *Syntax of Landscape: The Landscape Architecture of Peter Latz and Partners* (Basel: Birkhäuser Verlag, 2007).

Weller, Richard, *Room 4.1.3: Innovations in Landscape Architecture* (Philadelphia: University of Pennsylvania Press, 2005).

PICTURE CREDITS

2 Tom Fox, SWA Group; 10–12, 13 (left, above and below) Agence TER and Catherine Grandidier; 13 (right) Agence TER; 14–15 Yves Marchand and Romain Meffre; 16 (above, left and right) Agence TER; 16 (bottom) Yves Marchand and Romain Meffre; 17 (left) Alexandre Petzold; 17 (right, above and below) Yves Marchand and Romain Meffre; 19–20 Balmori Associates; 21 Pelli Clark Pelli; 23–25 Patrick Blanc; 27–31 Christopher Bradley-Hole; 32–37 Miran Kambič; 38–45 Fernando Caruncho; 46–48 Marion Brenner; 49 Andrea Cochran Landscape Architecture – Emily Rylander; 50, 51 Marion Brenner; 52–53 Geraldine Bruneel; 54, 55 Matteo Piazza; 56–59 estudioOCA; 71–75 Formwerkz; 76–79 Newtown Bagale GREENinc Momo; 80–83 GREENinc; 84–85 Guy Wernbone; 86–89 Renzo Delpino; 91–93 Anette Kisling; 94 (top) Patrick Altermatt; 94 (bottom) Hager Partner AG; 95 (top and bottom left) Rupert Steiner; 95 (bottom right) Patrick Altermatt; 97–101 Gisela Borghi; 103 Scott Shigley; 104 (top) Hoerr Schaudt; 104 (bottom), 105 Scott Shigley; 106–9 Hood Design; 110–15 Charles Jencks; 126–27 Mark LaRosa; 128–31 Charles Mayer; 132–37 Prabhakar. B. Bhagwat; 138–39 André Weisgerber; 140, 141 Michael Latz; 142, 143 Latz+Partner; 145–47 Tom Leader Studio; 149–51 Claas Dreppenstedt; 152–53 Jürgen Voss; 154, 155 Lohaus Carl; 156–59 McGregor Coxall; 160, 161 McGregor + Partners; 162–63, 164 (top) James Wilson; 164 (bottom) Mark McWilliams; 165 (top) Mesa Design Group; 166, 167 Tom Jenkins; 168, 169 (right) Charles Smith; 169 (left) Tim Hursley; 171–73 Chloe June Brown; 174–76 Daici Ano/Fwd Inc; 177 N-Tree; 178–83 Alejo Bague; 194–95 Paul Hester; 196 The Office of James Burnett; 197 (left) David Seide; 197 (right) The Office of James Burnett; 198–99 David Seide; 200–1 Y. Monel; 202, 203 Marianne Haas; 204, 205 Y. Monel; 206–9 Alexandre Bailhache; 210, 211 Tim Richardson; 212, 213 Sharon_K / Flickr Creative Commons; 214–17, 218 (left and middle) Syogo Oizumi / The Millennium Forest; 218 (right), 219 Midori Shintani / The Millennium Forest; 220, 221 Nicola Browne; 222–26 Péna & Peña Paysages; 228–30 Thomas Mayer; 231 Planergruppe Oberhausen; 233, 234 (bottom left) Liu Qihua; 234 (bottom right) Chen Bing; 234–35 (top) Pola / Jörg Michel; 235 (bottom) Chen Bing; 237 Patrizia Pozzi; 238, 239 Dario Fusaro; 250–57 Fernando Guerra and Sergio Guerra; 258–59 Michael Freisager; 260 Rico Rohner; 261 Raderschall Partner; 262, 263 Felix Brüngger; 264–67 Sant en Co; 268–69, 270 (top left and right) Nigel Dunnett; 270 (top centre and bottom), 272 (top left, top right, bottom right) Jane Sebire; 272 (bottom left) Nigel Dunnett; 273 Jane Sebire; 274–75 Nigel Dunnett; 276–81 Charles Mayer Photography; 282–87 Tom Stuart-Smith; 288–91 Marion Brenner; 292 Paul Rivera; 293 Surfacedesign, inc; 294, 295 Marion Brenner; 306–11 Tom Fox, SWA Group; 312–19 Turenscape; 320–25 Patrick Verbruggen; 327 Wette + Künecke; 328, 329 Steffen Spitzner; 331–33 Kim Wilkie; 334–39 Wirtz International; 340–43 ZUS (Zones Urbaines Sensibles).

ACKNOWLEDGMENTS

I would like to thank all of the designers and their teams for their assistance in the production of this book. The high quality of the photographs is testament to the expertise of the many photographers who provided images. I would also like to thank the designers and critics who provided submissions to the Forums in a spirit of common endeavour; their contributions are much appreciated.

I am grateful to Louisa Jones for her assistance with the translation of several texts in French. I was delighted to be able to work again with the 'dream team' of Myfanwy Vernon-Hunt (design) and Elain McAlpine (editor); once again, they have done a fine job. Finally, I would like to thank Lucas Dietrich, architecture and design editor at Thames & Hudson, for commissioning the book and then steering it along with wisdom and care.

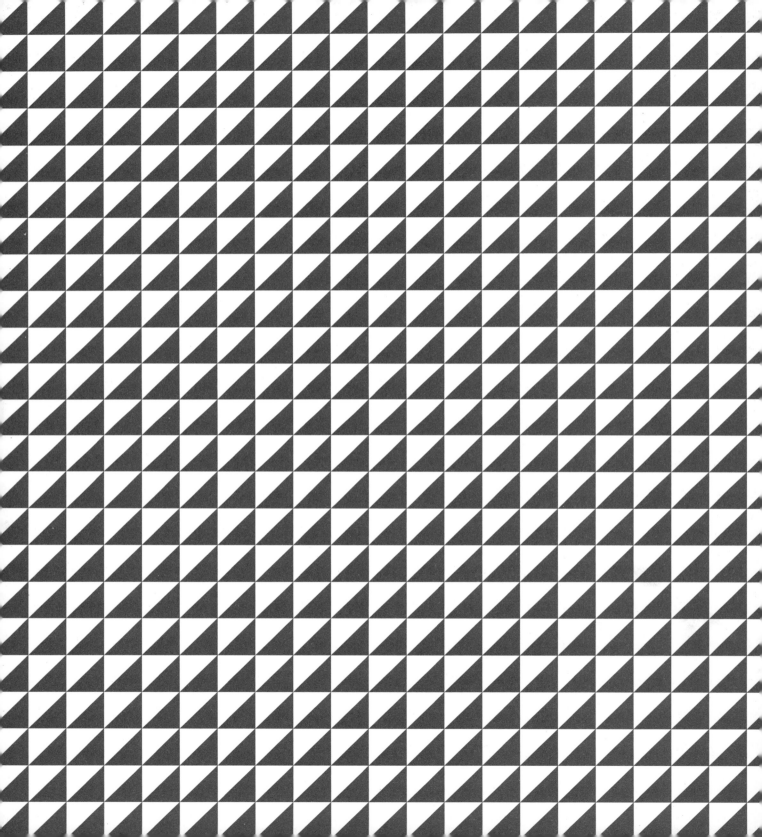